D1147819

PRESCRIPTION FOR ANXIETY

Books by Leslie D. Weatherhead

Published by Hodder and Stoughton
PSYCHOLOGY, RELIGION AND HEALING
HIS LIFE AND OURS
HOW CAN I FIND GOD?
PSYCHOLOGY AND LIFE
IT HAPPENED IN PALESTINE
A SHEPHERD REMEMBERS
THINKING ALOUD IN WAR TIME *
THIS IS THE VICTORY *
PERSONALITIES OF THE PASSION
IN QUEST OF A KINGDOM
WHEN THE LAMP FLICKERS
THE GUARDED UNIVERSE *
GUARDING OUR SUNDAY *
IS IT COURAGE WE NEED? *
A PRIVATE HOUSE OF PRAYER
THE RESURRECTION OF CHRIST
KEY NEXT DOOR AND OTHER CITY TEMPLE SERMONS
WOUNDED SPIRITS
THE CHRISTIAN AGNOSTIC

Published by the Epworth Press
AFTER DEATH
THE AFTERWORLD OF THE POETS
THE TRANSFORMING FRIENDSHIP
JESUS AND OURSELVES
PSYCHOLOGY IN THE SERVICE OF THE SOUL
THE WILL OF GOD
THE SIGNIFICANCE OF SILENCE
THE RESURRECTION AND THE LIFE
THAT IMMORTAL SEA
OVER HIS OWN SIGNATURE
A PLAIN MAN LOOKS AT THE CROSS *
SALUTE TO A SUFFERER

Published by the Student Christian Movement Press
THE MASTERY OF SEX THROUGH PSYCHOLOGY AND RELIGION
WHY DO MEN SUFFER?
DISCIPLESHIP
THE ETERNAL VOICE *

* *Out of Print*

PRESCRIPTION
FOR
ANXIETY

By
LESLIE D. WEATHERHEAD
C.B.E., M.A., Ph.D., D.Litt., D.D.

Minister-Emeritus, The City Temple, London
Formerly President of the Methodist Conference
Hon. Chaplain to Her Majesty's Forces

HODDER AND STOUGHTON

FIRST PUBLISHED 1956

NINTH IMPRESSION 1970

ISBN 0 340 01595 0

Printed in Great Britain for Hodder and Stoughton Limited, St. Paul's House, Warwick Lane, London, E.C.4, by Lowe and Brydone (Printers) Ltd., London

THIS BOOK IS DEDICATED TO

PERCY L. BACKUS
M.D., C.M., D.P.M.

E. HOWARD KITCHING
M.D., M.R.C.P., D.P.M.

and

A. DIXON WEATHERHEAD
M.D., M.R.C.P., D.P.M.

IN GRATITUDE AND AFFECTION

Acknowledgments

Special thanks are due for permission readily granted by:

Miss Erica Oxenham and Messrs. Longmans, Green and Co., Ltd. for John Oxenham's poem, "Shapeless and grim."

Mr. W. D. Kendall for quotation from his booklet, *The Conquest of Nerves.*

Messrs. Geoffrey Bles, Ltd., for quotation from *Surprised by Joy*, by C. S. Lewis.

Messrs. Macmillan and Co., Ltd., for quotations from *The Testament of Friendship*, by Vera Brittain and *Horizons and Landmarks*, by S. R. Lysaght.

Oxford University Press (Oxford Medical Publications) for quotation from *Dream Psychology*, by Maurice Nicoll.

Student Christian Movement Press Ltd., for quotation from *The Secret of Inward Peace*, by Herbert Gray.

Messrs. Doubleday and Co., Inc., for quotation from *The Conquest of Fear*, by Basil King (Copyright 1921 by Doubleday and Co. Inc.).

The Epworth Press for quotation from *The Meaning of Faith in Faith Healing*, by Denis Martin.

The World's Work (1913), Ltd., for quotation from *The Power of Positive Thinking*, by Dr. Norman Vincent Peale.

Messrs. John Murray Ltd., for quotation from *The Life of Edward Wilson.*

Messrs. Routledge and Kegan Paul Ltd., for quotation from *Neurosis and Human Growth* by Karen Horney.

CONTENTS

INTRODUCTION

To Whom it may Concern

THIS little book will not be the slightest use to a person who never worries and who does not know what it is to be plagued by anxious fears. It may be of help to people who are accused—and "accused" is the word because they are made to feel guilty—of having "nerves," of being worried and frightened and who are sometimes sleepless, and frequently depressed, weary and unhappy, especially in the mornings; who have vague fears, the origin and cause of which they cannot trace. The writer knows by experience what this feels like, and he would be happy to think that anything he had learned about coping with mental distress was of help to others who usually are entirely misunderstood by those who have never been through this particular hell of human misery.

We all know that the instinctive emotion called fear is frequently a friend rather than a foe. It is implanted in man's deep nature and we took it over from our animal ancestors. When they were in danger, fear caused certain glands to pour adrenalin into the blood and prepare the animal for "fight or flight."

When we cross the busy street, when we have been in contact with infectious disease, when we are chased down the country lane by an angry bull, and, in another phase of our life, when we are tempted to some wrong act, fear helps us to make the right reaction. Such fear is normal and valuable and we need not spend time discussing it.

Unfortunately we are frequently the victims of fears that are exaggerated and irrational, and yet we find it hard to get rid of them, even though we call ourselves "silly" when they attack us.   A grown man, whom I know, becomes frightened if he is in a room, especially a small room, and someone shuts the door.   This man is a fine Christian, but his faith seems powerless where his fear is concerned.   A grown woman I know would be terrified if she were called upon to pass alone through a dark wood.   She is a fine Christian also.   There are thousands of people who suffer from fears which are sent up into consciousness by emotional conflicts, or buried memories, or other factors so deep in the mind that the sufferer knows he is fearful, but does not know why.   Even now, the smell of paint induces in me a vague sense of fear because I had a frightening experience as a child in a room that was being painted.   Knowing the fact does not dispel the fear.   The situation has to be re-lived imaginatively and that is by no means easy to engineer, and does not always cure.

Scores of people who have confided in me through the years, have told me of childhood's fears at going to school— which I also suffered—and at going upstairs to bed in the dark.   They have spoken of fears of losing their dear ones, fears of failure, of meeting people, of insecurity, of illness, of old age, of death.   Thousands of people, as soon as they wake up, have a pang of terror and dismay at the thought of the day before them, and it does not pass away until half the day is done.   They pray about it, but it does not pass. Statesmen and politicians, "tough" business men and reserved women who never speak of their fears, are frequently bothered by them, whereas artists can sometimes be made physically ill by fears of failure touched off by the airy criticism of those who are totally unqualified to judge great art, whether it be painting, literature, architecture, sculpture, music or preaching.

If the mind is asked to endure such fears over a long period, it often tries to translate them into bodily illness. Perhaps as much as a third of the illness that fills our hospital beds is caused in this way. Many people do not get ill enough for this, but though able to carry on—which they do with immense courage—they never feel really well, and one would greatly like to help them so to understand how their minds may be working as to provide at least a measure of relief of mind and body through insight and readjustment.

In my opinion, the Christian religion offers positive help, but it is likely to be of maximum help only *after insight has been attained*, and anyone who uses this book as a "prescription" should follow this order. Prayer for healing in the case of a patient suffering from an abscess is more likely to be successful after correct diagnosis and surgical treatment. God can and does work miracles, but usually He asks for our co-operation. Bravely to track down the origin of our fears and to open them up and face them, however unpleasant and discreditable they may be, is often the first step to such co-operation. There is a story told of a witch who was turned into a cat. A small boy fled from it, terrified, only to find that it grew to the size of a calf and then to that of a house and followed him till he fell, unable to flee any further. But when he faced it and advanced toward it, it dwindled in size and finally ran under the door of the witch's cottage and disappeared. We must resolutely face our fears, not run away from them. We must work at ourselves, as well as call upon God and our friends to help us. "Work out your own salvation," said St. Paul, "*for it is God that worketh in you.*" We are exhorted to co-operate with God remembering that He is the Initiator of *our* effort, the Means by which it succeeds and the Goal at which it aims.

In this book I want to try to help people who suffer horribly from fears of one sort and another, who know the vague apprehension that eats away the heart, the fatigue and malaise set up in the body and the misery set up in the mind, and who have not got the time, or the means, or the opportunity to have analytical treatment at the hands of a psychiatrist—though in my opinion this is the best treatment—and who battle on day after day, frightened, unhappy and "nervy," easily depressed and upset, often despising themselves, and yet not knowing anything they can do about it. I want to offer what the Abbé Pierre called "penicillin for despair," and which he declared to be the world's greatest need.

Frequently nervy and frightened people are treated very cruelly. Their friends tell them to "pull themselves together"—whatever that means. They frequently feel that they have little strength to pull even if they knew what to pull on. They shrink into themselves and sometimes develop physical symptoms which some bluff and hearty physicians, who do not know how to treat them, call "all imagination," without realising that you can have a sick imagination as factually as an upset stomach, and it can cause you far more acute distress and unhappiness. Your emotions can be "ill" as well as your body, and they can cause in both body and mind a state of dis-ease.

I have blundered so often myself that I ought not to blame my fellow ministers for blundering, but I do wish that a healthy, hearty minister with a devoted wife and children, a happy home-life and a secure income, would not write, as one did in a newspaper recently, asserting that if you worried or feared, you were no Christian. What does he make of Christ in Gethsemane of Whom these words were written: "He began to be appalled and agitated"?[1] Dr. Vincent Taylor, a world-famous Greek scholar, says, "The verbs denote the distress which follows a great shock." And hundreds of thousands of British people are still suffering—though they may not realise it—from the shocks of the last war. After all, we were not made to be subjected to hot steel falling on us night after night from enemies in the sky, apart from the worse shocks of losing our dear ones by battle,

[1] Mark 14. 33 (Moffatt).

murder and sudden death. The minister wrote, "Any Christian can be serene." Was Jesus serene in the Garden when, "being in an agony" of mind, "His sweat became as it were great drops of blood falling down upon the ground"?[1]

If it is said that we never have anything as serious as that to face, I maintain that we little men have our little Gethsemanes and we do not want to be pushed yet further down into the pit of depression by being told that we are not fit to be called followers of Christ. Many of the fears we face have their origin in realms of the mind so deep that we have no control over them, and to rebuke the sufferer is like rebuking a man for having appendicitis or influenza. Indeed, some fears may come to us from the deep mind-pool which joins all minds together. Some fears may even have originated in our ancestors and have filtered through to us.[2]

Again, the fears of many are the fruit of their very assets, their experiences of the past, their vivid imaginations, their sensitiveness and responsiveness. "Sergeant, I believe you are afraid," said a soldier who had just reached the trenches and who had never previously been under fire. "Yes," said the sergeant, who was an old veteran and who knew all that could happen, "and if you were half as afraid as I am, you would go home." Many people must accept the fact that having experienced what they have experienced and being made as they are made, a certain amount of anxiety is likely to crop up from time to time whatever they do about it unless they can avoid all stress and strain.

Beyond doubt there are many unhappy people about. If they only knew that others have been where they are and that there are at any rate some things that can be said and done; if they only realised that they will not be told to "pull themselves together," or that they "imagine that they are

---

[1] Luke 22. 44.

[2] I have discussed this in *Psychology, Religion and Healing*, pp. 214-15 (Hodder & Stoughton, 4th Printing, 1954).

ill," even that would help. I have myself felt helped by disciplining myself to take the action suggested in this book; in other words, to take the medicine I prescribe. I do not pretend never to feel apprehensive. It is just that I have learned a few tips from friends that I think worth passing on, and I send out this little book in the hope that readers may find help also.

Frankly, it will not greatly help the reader merely to read the book. One does not just read a prescription. One gets it made up and takes the medicine. A reader who *acts* on the suggestions that follow will get the greatest benefit. One thing is certain: God understands us and will not cast us off however nervous and frightened we may be. But a quiet, persistent determination to win through, together with the help we can give each other, can save us from despair and prevent us from causing so much distress to our friends. At any rate, it is worth the attempt.

In writing this book I have had in mind the ordinary reader, not the student of psychology.

My wife, and my secretary, Miss Winifred Haddon, have once more given me unstinted help in preparing the book for the press, and I am grateful to my publishers for their unfailing courtesy and for some suggestions regarding the form which the book should take. I have dedicated the book to three psychiatrists who have given me immense personal help, but although they have all read the proofs and made useful suggestions, they are not committed to the points of view or opinions which I have expressed.

The City Temple,   LESLIE D. WEATHERHEAD
  London.

Easter, 1956.

Appendix I, "Everyman's House of Prayer", has now been extended into a book, "A Private House of Prayer", published by Hodder & Stoughton in two editions at 12/6d. and 16/-.

NOTE

ONE should not use the word "anxiety" without differentiating it from fear. Fear is a healthy emotion; a God-given response to danger.[1] Fear is the feeling that arises from a situation consciously threatening the welfare of the body, the mind or the soul, but *soluble by appropriate action*, as when we leap out of the way of a bus (body), are assured by a specialist that we have not developed cancer (mind), or are reconciled with God (soul).

Anxiety, on the other hand, is the feeling that arises when the welfare of the body, mind or soul is threatened by conflicting factors, conscious or unconscious or both, producing a situation *which cannot be solved by appropriate action* because of unconscious factors to which we have no direct access, or physical helplessness, or the scruples of conscience, or the fact that the terrifying situation is distant, either in space or time, and cannot be dealt with.

By a "neurosis" is meant a faulty, and sometimes disabling, emotional reaction to life at one or more points, with or without physical symptoms.

A patient with an "anxiety neurosis" feels afraid without being able to say what makes him afraid, or else he ascribes his fear to some cause which, for other people, would not be sufficient to cause so much fear as the patient feels.[2]

[1] See *Psychology and Life*, pp. 249 ff. *Psychology in Service of the Soul*, pp. 186 ff.

[2] See *Psychology, Religion and Healing*, pp. 499 ff.

I

SOME SYMPTOMS OF ANXIETY

I HAVE a deep sympathy for those who suffer from nervous apprehension, and I think I can help them, not from what I have read—though that often helps—or from what I have learned from the confidences of others—though that again has taught me a lot, especially the amount of secret courage there is in the world—but from my own experience of the same kind of darkness. For I, like many others, have had my dark valleys to go through, and when that has happened, I have received enormous comfort from friends of mine who *from their own experience* gave me advice and comfort, and, what I needed most, continual reassurance that the dark experience would pass and even be woven into the fabric of life, giving me insight into my own nature and making me better equipped to help others in their valley experiences.

First of all, we must put right away from our minds the thought that this time of darkness means that we have no faith, or that our religious experience is denied by our present symptoms. This is simply not true. Some of the greatest saints have known the deepest darkness and have survived the blackest nights. Christ Himself *felt* deserted by God and experienced in Gethsemane the stab of naked terror.

Secondly, do not let us feel that there is anything to be ashamed about in having nervous symptoms. No man has access to the unconscious part of his mind, or it would not be unconscious. Emotional conflicts can go on there and trip us up, however much psychology we know, just as a surgeon who specialises in heart disease can himself be the victim of it. Even conscious emotional conflicts can throw us into anxiety, especially when we cannot talk about them to anyone who really understands. A fear that we may be found out concerning a sin long repented of, may remain for years as a vague anxiety after its cause is completely forgotten. This anxiety can attach itself to almost anything and persist, for example, as a fear of disease.

If a child is shut up in a cupboard and is too frightened to pour out his fears, he may, even at a mature age, feel fear even at the thought of being shut in. I know grown men who are afraid of heights, or of darkness, or illness, or thunder, or knives, or even cats. How unfair, inaccurate and unkind it would be to say that if they had more faith, or more courage, or knew more psychology, they would be free! They are no more to be blamed for their symptoms than is an adult cripple who, when a child, met with some accident that made him lame. You can have a mind that limps as well as a body. Religion helps, but may not cure either the mind or the body without help of another kind as well, and not always even then. We must be very careful not to *reproach* people for their fears. We only add to their misery. We must not be content blandly to tell them to "have faith," for this merely deepens their depression and may give them the extra burden of a sense of guilt. Later we may be able to call out the faith they already have. That is what Christ did and we shall deal with that later.

Thirdly, while, in my opinion, the ideal treatment for anxiety is a series of interviews with a Christian psychiatrist, some cannot afford the money or the time, others are so placed geographically that such treatment is impracticable, and others again are too scared to try it or too old to expect much benefit. I write for those who live daily with fear, worry and anxiety.

When people tell me about insomnia and headache, a dry mouth and a palpitating heart; when they speak of that horrid feeling of a tight band round the head, or other form of constant headache, or of persistent fatigue and frequent trembling, of a kind of deadness of all feeling except fear, and of an inability to concentrate on anything but their own troubles, my heart goes out to them because I know all these symptoms at first hand. Indeed, I can remember wishing I had some physical illness to cope with that was more straightforward, and I think at times I would have accepted some killing disease. At least I thought so at the time!

Ideas even of a suicidal nature are not uncommon, but we can take comfort from the assurance that though they sometimes get into the "ideas-department" of the mind, they will not get into the "will-department." They are a trick of the mind, or rather *part* of the mind, which says, "I could get you out of your misery if you took my way." But that part of the mind cannot, thank God, do more than make suggestions, and in any case since we take our minds with us right *through* the experience of death, suicide is no escape, and we should have added cowardice to our depression and we should have brought pain and shame to our loved ones.

Deadness of feeling, even if we think we do not love anybody, not even God, must not make us worry. Love and trust still exist, but because the emotional machinery which registers them has gone wrong, we do not "*feel*" as we used to. But the machinery can, and will, be mended. Moreover, the truth that matters is not what *we* feel, but the *fact* that God loves us whatever we feel, and His energies are always tending towards our health and well-being.

> Let me no more my comfort draw
> From my frail hold on Thee;
> In this alone rejoice with awe—
> *Thy mighty grasp of me.*

Now what can we do about those symptoms? Well, a good doctor is generally able to give us something to alleviate them. Into this I am not competent to enter. But, apart from such help—which should not be ignored or neglected—I found the following advice useful.

1. Symptoms fade more quickly if we try to disregard them. We have had them before, lost them, had them again and lost them, and so on. On some days we may not have them at all. In other words, we have proved that they do pass, and they pass more quickly if we do not take them too seriously.

2. We must realise that part of our mind wants them. I know that sentence may sound silly. The reader will say, "He's wrong. I only want to be well." But those who really want to be well try to disregard their symptoms and try to act as though they were well. It is a good thing to begin "acting as though," even if it is "acting" that we ourselves can see through. This little bit of faith everyone possesses.

3. The part of our mind that wants symptoms is using them to make us escape, to run away, perhaps to retire from business, perhaps to escape into invalidism. But if those symptoms succeeded in making us do that, we should ultimately despise ourselves.

Moreover, the other part of our mind would give us hell—in terms of depression—for running away, and, when we recovered from these passing symptoms—and they *are* passing—we should want to kick ourselves for retiring. We should feel cowards, and cowardice costs more—in terms of depression and lost self-respect—than courage costs, though courage is harder.   Let us fight, then, against the conditions which cause depression, for one can even come to want it, to wallow in it, as if to say, "Pity me, love me, I am so unhappy."   Some people are reluctant to admit that symptoms have gone.   Part of the mind does not want to lose them.

4. When I was in this dark valley, I found that with almost a compulsion within me I wanted to tell my troubles to anyone who would listen.   And the reader who has shared this feeling may say, "Well, why not?   Surely I am entitled to a little sympathy."   Tell your doctor everything, of course, and a close friend or two—who may or may not include husband, or wife, or minister—*but not anyone else.*

And the reason is that if we talk a lot about symptoms, we give them *persisting power* and a spurious reality by paying attention to them.   They whisper continually, "Retire, withdraw, you are too ill to go on."   And really we are not nearly so ill as we feel.   The symptoms will pass, and we shall establish our whole life on a firmer footing by refusing to capitulate to mental pain.   It is easier to bear mental tension than the depression that follows capitulation.

It is not difficult to see why we want to tell others about our troubles.   We want sympathy because it is a substitute for love, and the mind needs love and approval as the body needs food and drink.   Especially we want the kind of sympathetic approval which we can get *without making the effort of changing at the points at which we have failed.* Sympathy is a form of approval we can get, however low our standard of achievement.   Thus we make our symptoms permanent by recounting them.   To get the sympathy for which we are hungry *we must retain symptoms.*   The healthy and well do not need sympathy.   Sometimes guilt sets up symptoms.   It is easier to bear the symptoms— which bring pity—than the self-despising caused by admitting guilt.   So the evil chain runs like this.   We tell our symptoms because part of our mind wants to keep them.

It wants to keep them to get pity. To get pity is more attractive and easier than to search for causes which may not be to our credit. The compulsion to retain the symptoms—because they bring pity—makes us retain the factors which cause the symptoms, of which guilt or escapism might be one.

To be loved truly and deeply and companionably is the only security the mind has. Failing that, we want the love (= sympathy) of others, and we want to get the soothing, but temporary, satisfaction which self-pity brings. But we must realise that every recital of our woes and every brooding hour etches on our minds the picture of the weaker, not the stronger, self: the self that cannot stick is out and *needs sympathy*; the self that is defeated, and that is the self we must cease to believe in because it is a false, masquerading self which, with no rights to the throne of our personality, is seeking to usurp it. That self is telling us we are ill, too ill to face life without running away, too tired to go on.

5. So let us cease from reciting our woes and symptoms except to the few who really can help us. When people say, "How are you?" say, "I'm getting on fine, thank you." If we regress to symptom-telling *we shall sell our courage to buy sympathy, and courage must be fought for at all costs*, for it pays a far higher dividend than sympathy or self-pity. We must not allow our symptoms to win the battle, but remember that the weaker part of the mind sometimes creates the symptoms to help *it* win.

No one who knows human nature will deny the reality of the battle. It is so much easier to clamour for, and to apply sympathy to the wounds we receive than to find out why and how we got wounded and to learn how to fight better. We accept sympathy because we are anxious, without facing the factors that make us anxious. Sympathy thus can become an anodyne for cowardice and for the pain which the recognition of cowardice would cause us.

Let us believe in the real, brave, healthy altruistic self and he will soon climb back on the throne of personality. When symptoms try to dominate, we may make ourselves write a letter of encouragement to someone in trouble, or go and call on someone in need, or do something with our hands, or walk in the country with a friend or give a child a treat.

The search for sympathy by recounting symptoms fixes in our minds, as certain chemicals fix the photographic negative, the permanent impression of ourselves as people needing sympathy—that is weak persons. We must dismiss that picture. Tear up that negative. It is a lie. It is not true of our real selves which can be strong and which can find and deepen their integrity by helping others in a thousand ways. Courage costs a lot, to put it mildly, but it makes us strong.

II

SOME CAUSES OF ANXIETY

As we challenge our anxieties and begin to move upward away from them, it is well to remember that we must not expect the graph of that progress to be a plain gradient constantly rising. It is a complicated path with dips and drops in it. It is not like this:

It is more like this:

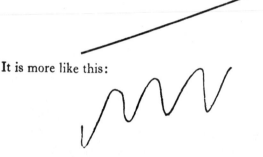

There will be days when we feel "blue" and we shall decide that we are no better. But even at the bottom of the "dips" we are higher than we were. We shall begin to have some symptom-free hours and even days, and they must make us believe that they will increase until nearly all the "dips" disappear. Those of us who are elderly and of the "anxious type" must not be discouraged if we have to reckon on *some* experiences of anxiety until the end. We must just accept them, recognise them as passing clouds and wait until the sun shines again as it certainly will.

What is true of the body is true of the mind. When we

cut our finger, a number of agencies immediately begin to produce healing, and when the mind is hurt or tired, there is a trend towards health and wholeness. We must co-operate, just as we get the dirt out of a cut, but God, or, as some prefer to say, the healing force of nature, is working with us for health. We must never forget that though God can use us whatever we are like, and weave our troubles, and even defeats and failures, into a wonderful pattern, He is on the side of health and healing. God is the perfect Artist, and no artist ever willed or intended imperfection in the creation of his art. Ill health is never the direct will of God in the sense that God desires it.[1]

Those whose lives are made miserable by anxious fears often ask why this horrid sense of terror descends upon them even when there is nothing in the immediate situation to account for the onslaught of fears.

They will often find that the symptoms of anxiety show themselves whenever self-esteem is threatened. Indeed anxiety has been defined by one American psychiatrist, Dr. H. S. Sullivan, as "that which one experiences when one's self-esteem is threatened." This definition is worth the closest scrutiny. Are we afraid of being found out? Are we getting old and revealing a frightening ineptitude? Are we afraid of failure? Are we over-sensitive to criticism?

Or perhaps the origin of our anxiety is much deeper.

The mind is a bit like a dark, deep pool. The surface, which I will call consciousness, is generally clear enough, but its stillness is broken sometimes by a bubble of gas rising from the bottom. A bubble is not much of a clue to what causes it. We should have to search the muddy depths to find out the cause, and that is what the psychiatrist seeks to do by his special techniques. If we "can't go in for all that" it won't hurt to do a bit of gentle probing.

Perhaps incidents that happened long ago, war experiences

[1] See my little pamphlet, *The Will of God* (Epworth Press, 1s. 6d.).

for instance, produced a lot of fear deep in the mind, and now something has stirred up the mud and set the fear free to disturb our conscious minds at the surface with bubbles of distress. I have known people who produced physical symptoms at the very memory of earlier frightening experiences.

Here is the case of a man tortured in adult life by fear. In his youth his father beat him repeatedly. More than once he was stripped naked, caned on the bare body, and then made to kneel down and ask God to forgive him for quite trivial failures to come up to his father's standard. That distorted his idea of God. God became linked with punishment and cruelty.

The attitude of the father made him afraid of being less than perfect. Whatever happened, *he* must not fail to achieve. He was even beaten when his school work was poor. That fixed in his mind a "pattern of reaction." *He feared that he might fail.* One of those severe beatings took place just after his mother died. It is easy to see the connection. His mother truly loved him and gave his mind comfort, reassurance and support. When she died, the fear of not achieving was unrelieved. Many years later, when his wife died, the man was faced with a sudden demand. He was invited to become a director of his company. Instead of joy at success, his dominating emotion was terror. *He might fail.* And there was no woman (= mother substitute) to reassure, comfort and sustain him. We can see where *his* fears came from.

There was a kind of emotional conflict going on in his mind. He desired that directorship and quite rightly. As the parable of the talents illustrates, it is not wrong to desire to use all one's powers in the fullest way. It is not wrong to want to make more money honestly. What one does with it is what matters in regard to honestly earned income. If money were in itself evil, Jesus would not have accepted the hospitality of rich folk, let alone have praised Abraham, who was one of the richest men in the Bible. It is not wrong to wield power and influence over others, though it is dangerous, and harder, whilst doing so, to remain humble.

But as soon as he made up his mind to accept the new post, there came into his mind also that old fear of failing. When he was a boy, failing meant the *fear* of punishment. So because he reacted to failure with fear as a child, he still reacted that way as an adult. If only his father had realised how terribly he was undermining his boy's self-confidence! If only he had known that on the tram-lines he laid down in childhood, the tram-car of his son's personality would run until his son was sixty, he would have burnt that wicked cane of his and silenced his critical tongue. Gradually the patient realised that the fears *had* that origin and the dead hand of the past lost its terrifying stranglehold on his personality. But fear, driven into the mind in childhood, can make people "anxious" for the rest of their lives.

I sometimes think that that is what Jesus was talking about in that fascinating interview with Nicodemus. He said, "You must be born again." Poor, obtuse, old Nicodemus said, "Can a man enter a second time into his mother's womb and be born?" But did not Jesus mean the very opposite of that, that we must cut free from the domination of our parents and live our own lives, born again of the water of new birth and the liberty-giving wind of God's spirit? Says a modern writer, "If the mother is possessive . . . if the son takes refuge from the grimness and dangers and problems of life by retreating again into the mother (his actual mother or some personal or institutional substitute), he will never find his own life, or in consequence be able to give his own love. He must undertake his own dark journey and be born anew."[1]

[1] Gerald Vann, *The Water and the Fire*, p. 68 (Collins).

B

A mother can imprison the ego of her child at an infantile level so that he never grows up emotionally. He follows the pattern which he developed in infancy. Mother love becomes "smother love". This is very serious, for the imprisoned ego will feel about God and *about other people whose approval he wants*, as he felt about his mother. He can become a sycophantic parasite, inwardly and unconsciously repeating to himself, "If I don't please, I shall lose love and this is a security I cannot do without." I know so many people who are grown up physically, but not emotionally. I think of one well known to me. Again and again he finds himself reacting to certain circumstances in the way that hardened into a "pattern of reaction" in very early days. Either he tries to appease people and make them like him by "charm," or if that will not work, he sulks with a sulk born of a hostility he is too frightened to show. Fear was sown in his nature in infancy, the fear that he would not be liked, and the fear that if he showed the resentment he felt, reprisals would follow.

We have all got to do what is very hard, namely to grow up and cut the spiritual umbilical cord. We are still "tied to mother," or, in other cases, father. We have not achieved our freedom. We must be born again.

I think of another friend who once confided to me some incidents that happened when he was sent by his firm to Hamburg. No one knows about them save God. No one ever will or can. And God has forgiven him. But when he told me about them, he still had a terrible sense of guilt. Half-buried guilt lies in the mud at the bottom of his mind and fear clings to it. He fears that others might get to know things. He fears that if the directors knew about them, he would be lowered in their estimation. His present fears come partly from a fear of exposure.

Religion has an important place to fill in such a case. God is all-forgiving and *therefore the patient must forgive himself.*[1] A friend of mine once said that if God puts our sins behind His back, we have no right to go behind His back, dig them up and wear them round our necks. A forgiven child can go ahead with a sense of freedom. The sin is cancelled.

> "He breaks the power of cancelled sin:
> He sets the prisoner free."

None of us is sinless. There is not one man living who has not done things he regrets. But remorse is useless and disintegrating. It has been called "regret without God." It might be a form of pride; an unreadiness to accept the fact that one is a certain kind of person since the events of one's life have proved it. Repentance is to go on to the glorious truth that, even so, God can do something with us if we commit ourselves to Him. Mere regret paralyses one from taking up the cudgels to fight the present and face the future. When we have repented and made restitution, the matter can be allowed to sink back into the mud. Even God will not stir it up against us, and it is robbed of its power to do us further harm and send up further bubbles of fear. Peter was made the chief of the Church, although Christ knew at the time what a wobbly sinner he was, and probably knew that one day Peter would wobble even more! But "this Man receiveth sinners," and we must not let either the events of childhood or the sins of manhood hamper any longer one made new in Christ, reborn by the spirit of freedom. One can say over and over to oneself, "I am loved, understood, forgiven and accepted." Let the past be a training that we leave behind like any other training. In future we will *use it*, but not regress to its tyrannies. It would not hurt a lot of people—not morbidly for hours at a time, but, say, while they are dressing—to look back into

[1] This point is worked out more fully in Chapter VII.

the past for events, especially the events of childhood, that may still be sending up to the surface of consciousness bubbles of fear for which they have never been able to account. A discovery of origin would help them to prick the bubbles and prevent them getting bigger, even if they could not dig up all the slime at the bottom of their mental pond.

When I was once passing through a very dark phase, due largely to physical illness— and of course when we are physically ill we all suffer both from a degree of anxiety and from regression to a more infantile level—I did not know whether to accept an onerous and very demanding position or withdraw from it. One day my wife said she thought the darkness could be part of God's training for the job. I came to accept that view. Fear itself can be *used* by God to equip us for our tasks, so long as we take the right attitude to it and do not let it cow us into surrender or into any of the many avenues of escape which the frightened mind suggests to us. I can only write down this simple testimony. Like all men, I love and prefer the sunny uplands of experience, when health, happiness and success abound, but I have learned far more about God and life and myself in the darkness of fear and failure than I have ever learned in the sunshine. There are such things as the treasures of darkness. The darkness, thank God, passes. *But what one learns in the darkness, one possesses for ever.* "The trying things," says Bishop Fenelon, "which you fancy come between God and you, will prove means of unity with Him, if you bear them humbly. Those things that overwhelm us and upset our pride, do more good than all that which excites and inspirits us."

III

HOW THE BODY REFLECTS THE MIND'S ANXIETY

THE word "anxious" is used to express both fear and desire. "I am anxious about you," expresses fear. "I am anxious to meet you," expresses desire. We must be alert to challenge the fear that gives us trouble because it is in conflict with desire. The mind can more easily stand a big strain made on it if the "pull" is all in one direction. What the mind finds it harder to stand is the conflict of being pulled one way by fear and the opposite way by desire. This produces what psychologists call an "anxiety state." Sometimes the factors which cause such a state are pushed down into the unconscious part of the mind, or are partly conscious and partly unconscious. If the conflict is not faced and dealt with, it can cause breakdown, and, if its factors are unconscious, psychiatric help generally becomes necessary.

At the same time, much can be done to overcome anxiety by those willing to be ruthlessly honest with themselves and to recognise, as far as they can, what is troubling them. Here is a man who desires to accept a responsible post because of its prestige and salary, but fears he cannot hold it down and will fail. His self-esteem is threatened and he develops anxiety. Here is a girl who desires to be a missionary, but fears that people will accuse her of deserting an aged mother and father. Here is a girl who desires marriage and a home, but fears sex, and whose anxiety symptoms show up every time she is with her lover. Here is a man who desires to express the emotion of anger or aggression, but fears hostility or the withdrawal of love. Here are countless elderly people troubled more than they have ever realised by the conflict between desire to maintain their old standards of efficiency and the fear that the inevitable ageing process is diminishing their ability in ways that are now beginning to show. Short of psychiatric help we can courageously try to understand such symptoms, for understanding leads to victory.

Trembling is one of the symptoms. It is caused sometimes by the conflict between the desire to run away and the fear of being labelled coward and of letting oneself and others down—say by giving up one's job. Understanding helps. Understanding can lead us to realise that it is worthwhile and possible to carry on, and beneath one's dignity and self-respect to run away. This torment of the divided self appears as a devil in many disguises of which trembling is one. Hypochondria, headaches, backaches and other pains are sometimes others. Even understanding may not stop our trembling. In that case we must *accept the tremble* and carry on like the brave old Marshal Turenne of France who sacrificed so much that he might maintain his Christian Protestant witness. When he was shaving just before a battle, his hand trembled violently, and he turned on his own body and said this: "Tremblest thou, vile carcass? Thou would'st tremble more if thou knewest where I am going to take thee this day!" But though he trembled, he went on. One of the bravest men I ever knew, a commando in the war, who at twenty-three was a major with a D.S.O., and an M.C. with bar, told me himself that in every adventure he trembled and felt his mouth go dry and his knees shake.

I think of many people I have known who have been caught in conflicts, some conscious, some unconscious, and they have endured the torment of *desiring* to run away without running away, until finally the devil of fear left them, and the angels of comfort and a new self-respect and sense of power came and ministered to them.

If the devil can make us ill or always morbidly troubled

about our health (hypochondriasis), he has got us where he wants us because he makes us say, "I'm so ill I must retire." We must believe in the real self and it will get strong.   We must recognise and laugh at the devil who says, "Run away, retire, withdraw."   Devils hate being laughed at.

Fatigue is another common symptom of anxiety.   It may be caused by the fact that so much energy is used up in holding down fear and anxiety in the unconscious depths of the mind (rather like keeping a football under the water of the pond (p. 27)), that there is not enough energy left over with which to face the ordinary demands of life.

Fatigue is *sometimes* brought on by a bit of the mind saying, "Retreat, you are not well enough to face life."   Sometimes it cloaks sheer cowardice.   It is easier for the mind to tolerate tiredness than to admit cowardice, and, of course, tiredness leads to self-pity, and often the sympathy of others, so that we can be cowards and yet not lose our self-respect and self-love.   Sometimes fatigue is set up by our attempts to remain on some pedestal of achievement or some position in the public eye when failing health or moral weakness proves that the pedestal must be evacuated.   We fear the loss of self-esteem by such evacuation.   We want public approval and praise and will not be honest even with ourselves.   Real, physically caused fatigue, vanishes with rest, but this spurious sham goes on and on until it is challenged and seen through, or until we really *want* to do something.   Then it can go within the hour.   I have proved the truth of this myself.

Emotional fatigue is different.   I find it attacks me before and after preaching or after listening too long to other people's troubles.   Nervousness and sympathy make one's muscles tense and thus tired.   If one cannot learn how to relax one must get exercise in the fresh air.   One often *feels* too tired to do this, but if one persists, one can exchange the wretched emotional exhaustion for a physical one which can *then* be treated by rest.

We have got to watch continually the power over the body possessed by that bit of the mind that wants to make us run away and hide either in illness or some other escapist device. Often I find myself out in this matter. Saturday is my day for producing symptoms! I should be treated with much kindness on Sunday if I could say I had "not been feeling well yesterday." So the desire to do well and the fear of failure make a conflict. I become "anxious." Then that traitorous bit of mind tries to soften the blow of possible failure by producing symptoms which enable me to say to myself, "I *should* have done well if I had felt better." What traitors wait within us! How many soloists have a sore throat at the last minute, hoping the listener will feel, "Well, if he can sing like that with a sore throat, how wonderful he must be when he is really well!" How often the mind seeks to ward off attacks on our self-esteem by producing symptoms which we hope will evoke the pity of those who might criticise us, including ourselves!

The appearance of suspicious symptoms should make us ask honestly what that traitor bit of mind is likely to *gain* by producing them. Psychologists always say to themselves, "What does the patient gain by having these symptoms?" They know that the traitor-mind wishes us to be ill enough to escape a difficulty which—because of some inner weakness —we cannot solve, and they know that patients often feel a need to punish themselves for that weakness. A symptom sometimes provides a means by which we can evade a difficulty and have an excuse for evasion. Sometimes the symptom provides us with sympathy, or pity, or affection for which we all crave. Sometimes a symptom enables us to "maintain face" and not see ourselves as cowards, or be seen to be such by others. Sometimes fear itself disappears when a really serious physical condition develops. That coward bit of mind does not need to produce a headache, if you have been run over by a taxi! So many illnesses and the results of accidents are maintained for long periods because they serve that little traitor-bit of our minds. Research has been done on what is called "accident-proneness" because some people seem much more likely to "have an accident" if the accident or its effects would serve a compensatory purpose. I do not mean that they consciously invite accidents. The unconscious mind is trying to help them end their anxieties by getting them out of their difficulties. Its purpose and method are unconscious. Sometimes that purpose is the need for punishment which part of the mind demands as the price of setting us free from guilt feelings. If so, there is no treatment to compare with the Christian gospel of God's forgiveness.

Often when we have become free from the symptoms which fear imposes, we shall find that returning to work after a holiday imposes a special strain. That bit of mind which I have called "the traitor" is saying, "You are not yet well enough to face the strain," or, "You cannot maintain your old standards," or, "You are still overtired from earlier strains," or something of the kind. This is a crucial time, and the way to meet it is, I think, by asserting the true picture of oneself as I suggest in Chapter V. "I *can* carry on for now I am different. These symptoms are a bluff and I can see through them," is the attitude to take. We shall then see returning symptoms as a cheeky attempt of the "traitor-mind" to rationalise escape from responsibility. Escape is always easier than fighting. But if we make that new picture of ourselves every morning, then the growing sense of power will make us feel disgust and nausea at the old habit of reciting symptoms. The real self which is in eternal communion with God will banish the traitor and reign.

As for that depression, it will go also, and the sooner we *really* want to part with it the better. It is sometimes useful for us to ask ourselves whether it would not go at once if someone came into the room whom we especially wanted to have a good opinion of us, or if a little child—whom we would not dream of inflicting with depression—sought our aid. Is it sometimes a thing we wallow in so as to hurt others? We should check up on whether we feel, "I'm depressed, and you needn't think you can get me out of it. I'm going to maintain it to get your sympathy and affection, and if you don't give it me soon, I may do something desperate, and then you *will* be sorry for me." It is easier to sink into depression than to take courageous action, ignoring how we "feel."

It helped me to get rid of depression when it dawned on me that though I was hungry for love, it is the love one *gives* that brings a far deeper satisfaction than the love one receives. I hate the idea of saving one's own soul by serving another, and yet isn't there something in it? I have always felt a bit better if I could go and see someone who was a bit worse than myself, especially, as is so often the case, when the people we visit show more courage over their major disasters than we do over our minor ones. Visiting others takes one's mind off oneself, for one thing, and switches it from negative thinking into positive, and that is a vastly important thing to do.

I read somewhere of a man who tried to cure himself of negative thoughts by giving his wife sixpence every time he uttered a negative thought. He found he had quite a lot to pay up at the end of a day! She pounced on him if he only said he was afraid it was going to rain! If he said he was afraid he wasn't going to sleep that night, she was on him like a ton of bricks, and if he said he thought he was going to be ill, she wanted double pay! Slowly he found the value of thinking positively. He *expected* health. He *expected* a serene, confident, joyous day from the moment he awakened. Thus he found a way of life that left no *anxious* thought for the morrow. The discipline of positive thinking helped to change his whole life.

I once knew a man who stuck slogans all over his own desk. I used to tease him about them, but now I think he was very wise. They were all positive affirmations like: "I can do all things through Christ Who strengtheneth me," or "Lo, I am with you always, even unto the end of the world." It is a good idea to have a card up on the shaving mirror with some new positive idea for each day or for each few days.[1] We should all advance more quickly out of our dark valleys if we disciplined ourselves to throw out of our minds all negative and fear-full ideas and substituted positive affirmations of what God has promised.

Insomnia is one of the most unpleasant symptoms of anxiety. Here the doctor can help us with the temporary use of drugs. Some people refuse them on principle, but I would take a stick and have iron spikes in my shoes if I were crossing a glacier, and I do not see why an anxious person should not have help while crossing a slippery place in his mental life which is imposing on him a greater strain than usual. I know what the long, drawn-out misery of sleepless nights is like, and a wise doctor can soon get us off the use of a drug when we are over the difficult place. One doctor advises his patients not to toss restlessly in bed and wait until one or two in the morning and then take a sleeping-pill, but to take one regularly for a week or two on getting into bed and make sure of a good night, and then, having restored the rhythm of sleeping, slowly reduce the amount, and, if possible, go for a holiday until the patient forgets to take the pill and finds he does not need it, except perhaps after an unusually mentally strenuous or exciting day.

The greatest help I got about not sleeping, however, was the word of a specialist that lying awake does not really harm us. It is worrying about not sleeping that does the harm.

[1] My friend the Rev. Gordon Powell of Sydney, Australia, has worked out this idea most usefully. See his book, *Happiness is a Habit* (Hodder & Stoughton).

If we lay relaxed and quiet, we should not lose much by not losing consciousness. Even during unconsciousness the deep mind is busy, as our dreams show. One can have a night made more exhausting by dreams than by lying awake. We toss and fume and say to ourselves, "I shan't be any use tomorrow if I don't get some sleep," and the fretting does wear us out, whereas to lie awake without being concerned about it, is harmless and incidentally is an attitude that often woos and wins sleep. Another bit of comfort I got was to find that many people over fifty find that five-and-a-half to six hours of sleep each night suffice.

One cannot hope to write helpfully about all the symptoms which fear can set up in the body. Various aches and pains that have no origin in a physical situation are notoriously "psycho-somatic." It is a wonderful word, but means that though the pains are in the body, their origin is in the mind. Again and again, emotion that one cannot express openly, and may not even recognise as existing at all, can be translated into physical pain. It is worth asking oneself whether in our minds there is any anger, or fear, or resentment, or hate, or sense of guilt, or frustration that we are not permitting to come up into consciousness and which is being translated into bodily symptoms. But if any pain persists and the doctor is certain that it has no physical origin, I should advise a few talks with a good psychiatrist. If these take place, the patient must be ready to be utterly honest with him and not worry about what he thinks of one. If he is a good psychiatrist, he will be out to heal, not to judge, and it is silly to pretend to him. By "coming clean" we give him a chance to help. In any case no good psychiatrist sets up as an arbiter of his patient's morals.

To talk as I have done about trembling and fatigue and insomnia is inadequate, but it helps a bit to know that other people have had all these troubles and come through them. Symptoms will seem increasingly unimportant as we gain insight into their cause, and as we work hard on ourselves to eradicate the causes and *really* trust God. Says Dr. Denis Martin, in a valuable pamphlet costing only a shilling,[1] "We can define the faith-experience as a step-by-step commitment of the entire self, and as the outcome of a relationship which reveals progressively the all-loving nature of God, and so inspires increasing trust and confidence. The result of this experience is, in its turn, a progressive liberation of the personality from fear and anxiety, as real awareness increases that we are loved and accepted by God no matter what aspects of ourselves are brought to light."

I know how symptoms can so irritate us that we even long to die. Here we may listen to a great and brave man, Edward Wilson, who went with Scott to the South Pole: "It is not a sin to long to die, the sin is in the failure to submit our wills to God to keep us here as long as He wishes. . . . Rise above your difficulties—be sorry for them through whom your difficulties come to you. In refusing to be put out and annoyed, you are taking God's hand in yours, and once you feel God's hand, or the hand of anyone that loves good, in yours—let *pity* take the place of irritation, let *silence* take the place of a hasty answer, let the longing to suffer in ever so small a way take the place of a longing to rest."[2]

[1] *The Meaning of Faith in Faith-Healing*, pp. 12–13 (Epworth Press, 1954).

[2] George Seaver, *Life of Edward Wilson*, p. 72. (John Murray, 1933).

IV

THE TRUTH ABOUT GOD LESSENS ANXIETY

MANY people are puzzled because their religion does not help them more in those dark days known only too well by all who suffer with their "nerves." Depression can be so deep and desolate that to pray is the very last thing one feels one can do. At such times, it is good advice to say, "Don't try to pray. Sit back and let your friends pray for you." In a time of depression it is the turn of one's real friends to pray for one, to stand by one and to tell one—what is certainly true—that not only will one get through this dark valley, but that God will weave all this suffering into His pattern.[1] I do not mean He sent the suffering. That, I hold, is never true. It comes to us from the evil in the world; the product of ignorance, or folly, or sin in ourselves or more often in the great human family with which we are bound up; a family whose assets enrich our lives and whose liabilities we have to bear and share. But God will use our suffering to give us such insights into life and into His ways with men as will spell immense progress and usefulness later. This kind of suffering brings a new quality of unmorbid, sincere and positive sympathy for others, unpossessed by those who have never known this darkness, and we are never too old to profit by it, for we are going on for ever. This earth-life is only the lowest form in God's school. We have got a lot of schooling to go through before we are perfected; before

---

[1] The question, "Why does not religion help more?" is discussed more fully in Chapter X.

we can have anything like full communion with Him, and I suppose it was for this that we were created at all, for His joy and our bliss, that bliss being the perfect fulfilment of our being, through our life in Him. It will be grand at last to stop thinking of ourselves, and both lose and find ourselves in His perfect splendour and glory.

Many people tell me that they know they ought to trust God, but in fact they do not. I applaud their mental honesty. That is good, for the first law of mental health is to be ruthlessly honest with oneself. I feel so sympathetic with those who find trusting God difficult that I will devote this chapter to the subject.

Because of countless disappointing experiences, confidence is harder to maintain, as one gets older. I have confirmed this with many of my friends, and, for myself, recall that in my twenties, during part of the First World War, I lived with the Arabs out in the wilds of the desert, where dangers were all around, and I had no idea at all where I was, yet I could lie down in my sleeping-bag under the stars and sleep quietly all night. Sleeping-pills were unknown to me in my youth. Far less dangerous situations can now hinder sleep, and on inquiry I find that many people—especially elderly people—fight an almost ceaseless battle against fears which in youth never bothered them.

If this is so, let us ask ourselves why our trust in God is not more firmly founded. It is quite easy for us to trust our friends. If it were in their power, they would help us. We could repose the utmost trust in them. Why, then, is it so hard really to trust God? For we sing a lot about trusting Him and we try to do it, but many of us would trust almost anyone or anything else first!

Without doubt, a child makes his picture of God from the adults who dominate his childhood. My own home was one of very severe discipline and as a child I hated and dreaded school because the teachers resorted to the cane on the slightest pretext. Being a shy and delicate child, often away with illness when new lessons were learnt, I came in for innumerable beatings. Side by side with this I put the stories I have heard from others. For instance, I received a letter recently from a woman who said that she always feared God because she was told as a child that when there was a thunderstorm it meant that God was angry with her. So fearful was she that she hid in a dark cupboard and sang hymns hoping to appease the angry deity! At the end of a year she was told that God was so angry with her naughtiness in the year that had fled, that He would probably not give her another to try in. She writes, "I used to lie awake alone and listen, and I can remember the joy I experienced when I heard the church bells ringing in the New Year— and *I was still alive.*" Thousands of people of my generation have been frightened with stories of hell-fire, and tens of thousands have been told, "If you aren't a good boy, Mummy won't love you," and worse still, "If you aren't a good boy, *God* won't love you." Indeed, children make the latter a deduction from the former.

I am afraid the Church is also to blame for false teaching about God. It so stresses morality above love that a man who falls morally generally leaves the Church, when the Church should consist of loving and understanding people dedicated to the task of the sinner's recovery to self-respect. The Church should be the loving, forgiving, understanding, accepting and restoring community. The anxiety patient dreads rejection and is likely to transpose the rejection by the Church to rejection by God. An unloving Church may increase his anxiety.

My own picture of God, and the pictures of thousands, were made out of stern parents, or angry school-teachers, or fierce, denunciatory preachers with an added element of a great big policeman, or Gestapo official, or angry potentate. So our attitude to God is that we must appease Him if we can, and be good so that He will love us, together with a kind of submerged and frightened aggression; submerged because boys cannot openly be aggressive to their parents or teachers lest they receive further punishment.   The attitude to God of many is that He will not love them unless they maintain His very difficult and high code of ethics, and underneath a pretence of love is fear and sometimes even hate.

Children have so often been made to feel that their parents will not love them unless they are good that inevitably they project on to their heavenly Father the feelings they have developed about an earthly father and mother.   Thus they try to solve the problems of their relationship to God by attaining an ethical standard quite beyond them, and they break down, or else give up both the quest for perfection and the worship of their self-made God.   They cannot believe in UNCONDITIONAL LOVE, but only in a love which depends on the attainment of moral standards.   This morality-obsession gets in the way of their love-relationship with God and pushes those who do not give up religion altogether into the law-relationship between the elder brother and his father in the story of the Prodigal recorded in Luke 15.[1]   "I have been good," says the elder brother in effect, "therefore I have the right to security."   The glorious truth is that God loves us whatever we do and our "rights" are the rights of a love-relationship, that of sons and heirs, not the right born of achievement in the moral realm.   We fail to put our trust in the inherent, redemptive quality of love alone.   If we did, moralising would be unnecessary.   We should hate to break a relationship with One Who loved us as God does.   Our picture of God is wrong.   It is that of a tyrant.

Now if we have such a tyrannical God as that, Who of

[1] See especially verses 28–30.

course is not the true God at all, but a bogey, how can we possibly trust Him? Many of us need to realise that our picture of God, as strict and punishing and disapproving, is not God, but a caricature we made as children. No one can possibly commit himself to a God Whom he fears in that way. Fear completely kills trust, and frankly I believe that that is why hosts of people do not really trust God. Indeed, *their* God is not to be trusted. No wonder one man could write to me and say, "God has never been any use to me." I replied that his God would not be of any "use" to anyone, but that fortunately for the world his God was not the real God, but only a figment of his own distorted imagination.

All this is tied up with the "will-of-God-heresy." I cannot imagine how people can suppose that the cruel and horrible diseases that fall upon them are the will of God in any intelligent sense of the word. Who can trust a God Who snatches a dear young wife and companion away by giving her a foul disease that eats away her beautiful body? Who is likely to trust a God Who any moment may snatch away a young husband at a time when he is just holding together his little family of wife and three young children? Who can trust a God Who, to teach her that He is a loving Father (!), deliberately wills that a bright, healthy girl of fifteen, a hockey player and a lover of open-air swimming, shall develop polio and lie for months with twisted and useless limbs? If one "*wills*" anything, one *wants* it to happen. No one but a fiend could look upon a polio or cancer victim and say, "That is what I *wanted* to happen." Who can trust a God Who, as soon as a young surgeon has qualified, "wills" blindness in both eyes so that he cannot do even his first operation? This was a case actually known to me and I could give scores of others. Frankly, I would not worship or trust a God like that for five minutes, and to love Him is impossible. Jesus repudiated this idea with vigour and spoke of a woman who had been ill for many years as one "whom Satan hath bound."[1] That is better. Let us call it Satan, as Paul called his chronic illness.[2] Let us call it man's ignorance, or folly, or sin, or let us call it, if you like, the impact of evil intelligences or of the Devil himself. But let us not label a thing "the will of God" for which a man would be sent to a criminal lunatic asylum for the rest of his life. Let us keep the phrase "the will of God" for those things which God *intends* to happen, not for those things which, because He allows evil, God allows to happen. God is the great Artist of the universe and no artist intends imperfection like disease in the created object. What potter would create a vase and *intend* a flaw in it?

We get to the point, then, at which in their secret hearts people say, "If God will let us alone, we shall be all right." They secretly fear that He will *send* them some horrible disease or a nervous breakdown, and that the Church will ask them to label it "the will of God," and ask them to trust Him. All this false thinking we must shed without delay. "No one will ever be released from fear by clinging to the teachings which have inspired fear. We are fearless in proportion as we grow independent enough to know for ourselves."[3]

Now let me say four things:

1. We certainly need God as much as man ever did, for if ever there were a world over-clouded with fear, this is it.

---

[1] Luke 13. 16.

[2] II Corinthians 12. 7.

[3] Basil King, *The Conquest of Fear* (Doubleday, New York, 1953), to whom I am indebted in this chapter.

We have a new horror in the hydrogen bomb and the possibility of a third war on top of all the other horrible catastrophes that can happen to us. We know that Jesus lived the loveliest life ever lived on earth, and we know that He could not live without God. How then can we? Life without God just does not make sense to me. Except for occasional experiences it is more like a cruel and heartless trick played on us by a fiend and without purpose or significance.

As the scientist Whitehead says, "The fact of the religious vision . . . is our one ground for optimism. Apart from it, human life is a flash of occasional enjoyments lighting up a mass of pain and misery."[1]

2. We must have the real God, not a bogey made out of father, or mother, or a preacher, or a policeman, or a judge, or the Gestapo, or some vindictive eastern potentate. In other words, we must look at Jesus and go on looking until we really believe that nothing is true of God, even if it is in the Bible, unless it is in harmony with the character of Christ. Then, and only then, can we rejoice in the Lord and delight ourselves in Him, as the Bible exhorts us to do.

3. We must especially realise that God's love is in no way lessened by our moral failures. *We* may break the relationship, but He never withdraws His love. That is very hard for some people to accept, but the real God does not say, "If you are not a good boy, Father won't love you." We have not got to appease God, or buy His love, or try to earn it. We cannot in any case deserve it or win it. We can only kneel down and humbly accept it. But it is ours to be claimed *whatever we have done and whatever we are still like.* Listen to Jesus! "He maketh His sun to rise upon the evil and on the good, and sendeth rain on the just and

---

[1] A. N. Whitehead, *Science and the Modern World,* p. 238 (Camb. Univ. Press).

the unjust."[1] The volume of love that falls upon us—if one may put it thus—is the same whether we be saints or sinners. "He is good to the thankless and the evil."[2] Didn't Jesus say, "Love your enemies and do good to them that do evil to you," and didn't Paul say the same? So even if we rebel against God and make ourselves His enemies; if we are seething with rebellion against God, He does not alter His attitude or withdraw His love. He is not so mean as to weigh up our worthiness and decide whether to love us or not. He loves us equally whether we are sinners or saints. He will never do us an evil, or let an evil which befalls us have the last word. If He must not divert it or deliver us from it yet, He will make it serve us and serve His purpose in us and for us. His omnipotence does not involve that everything that happens to us is His *will*, but it does involve that nothing can possibly defeat Him ultimately.

4. He will love us with this steady, purposeful, goal-seeking love *for His name's sake*. God will not lose His good name as a God worth trusting by doing things as despicable—considering His power and our feebleness—as would be the action of a boy who pulled the wings off a fly, or that of a fourth form, devil-possessed youngster I read of, who cut off his puppy's ears because it would not learn a trick he tried to teach it, or that of another depraved boy who put a live kitten into the oven. Yet these revolting pictures are mild compared with the pictures of hell which some minds still retain.

Without doubt hell is a reality. I have glimpsed it myself and through the eyes of others I have seen it often.

---

[1] Matthew 5. 45. Prof. C. C. Torrey translates Matt. 5. 48 as follows, and I think rightly, "Be ye therefore all inclusive in your goodwill even as your Heavenly Father includes all in His goodwill." The simile of the sunshine and rain falling on all suggests impartiality rather than perfection and though we are to aim at the latter, much anxiety has been set up by those who demand it in themselves or others as the *condition* of God's love.

[2] Luke 6. 35.

But we make it ourselves. We can wander away from the only path that will bring us home, and get lost in the dreary, dark jungle of self-centredness in which we are separated from God by our own sins, but as the *Theologia Germanica* says somewhere, "Nothing burneth in hell but self-will; therefore it hath been said, 'Put off thine own will and there will be no hell.'" Hell is a state of mind created by the self, organised around itself instead of being organised around God, but the path back from that jungle is always discoverable, the door of God's home is always open and so are the Father's arms. No man will go to hell who does not send himself there by finally saying "No" to God and finally shutting the door against love.

Every springtime the tiny fledgling birds creep to the edge of the nest and look over and—unless I am projecting my own feelings on them unfairly—shrink back from the abyss below the nest. They imagine that the strength of their own wings is the only factor that can save them from death, and how feeble those wings are! Yet, when they launch away, or, as in the case of some birds, are pushed over the edge, they will find when they spread their wings that *the air itself supports them.* Is not God just like that supporting air? How can He keep His good name if we commit ourselves to Him and are utterly destroyed, remembering that many things look like catastrophe, feel like catastrophe and are called catastrophe that afterwards turn out to be very different? Or to change the figure, if God is really utterly beneficent—and this I truly believe—then He is like a great river of loving purposefulness. We are to plunge in without trying to swim even with the current, let alone against it, and just keep our head above water and face the way the river is going. If we utterly commit ourselves to His way and do our best, then the responsibility of our arrival at the goal of His purpose for us is His, not

ours. We are unsure of ourselves and there is certainly no
security anywhere in the world, but we can be utterly sure
of Him.

We do not need a lecture on psychology to tell us that
courage is not the virtue of those "who do not know what
fear is." I do not believe there are such people. Jesus
was in an agony of fear in the Garden and those hours
come to us all. Courage is possessed by the man who
estimates the fear-causing situation, but summons all his
resources and meets it. Courage comes by doing courageous
things when we want to run away, and let us remember that
a little child going upstairs to bed in the dark and imagining
all sorts of bogeys and horrors, often shows as much courage
as a soldier whose impulsive dash during some peak of
mental excitement wins him a medal for bravery.

So let us, fifty times a day if need be, set before us a
picture of *the real God*, utterly loving, whatever we have done,
infinitely strong, resourceful and purposeful, finding this
way for us when that way is closed for whatever reason,
Who will not allow us to be lost and defeated if we trust
Him, and Who is generous beyond all thoughts of generosity.
Let us commit ourselves to Him every morning, for the
real God is to be trusted, and whatever happens to us—
called, as it may be by men, failure, catastrophe or defeat—
we shall know that eternal Love still bears us on its bosom,
and that we shall find our way home without regret.

> I will not ask what joys or woes
>   Time holds for me;
> I'll simply seek a love that goes
>   Out unto Thee,
> As surely as the river flows
>   To meet the sea.

V

THE TRUTH ABOUT OURSELVES
LESSENS ANXIETY

I REMEMBER reading about an Edinburgh weaver who repeatedly offered this unusual prayer: "O God, help me always to keep a good opinion of myself." It would not be the right prayer for some people, but for those given to a too fierce disparagement of themselves, it would be the right prayer to offer. Jesus told us to love our neighbours *as ourselves*, which involves a belief in ourselves, a picture of ourselves as lovable. If God loves us in the way Jesus reiterates over and over again, in His words about the lilies and the sparrows[1] and in His parables of the lost sheep, the lost coin and the lost son,[2] then to despise and overblame what God loves, is to pit our judgment of values above His. Samuel Johnson remarks somewhere to Boswell that the ordinary doings of an ordinary man become of world-wide interest if he becomes the friend of a world-famous man. If this were not true, Boswell himself would never have been heard of. However trifling we may feel ourselves to be in God's great universe, it is worth remembering that "when a King picks up a trifle, it is a trifle no longer." God sent His Son to "pick us up" and He loves us, understands us, forgives us, accepts us and believes in us. If, therefore, we have in our minds a picture of ourselves as fear-haunted and defeated nobodies, we must get rid of that picture at once and hold up our heads. That is a false

[1] Matthew 6. 26.
[2] Luke 15.

picture and the false must go. God sees us as men and women in whom and through whom He can do a great work. He sees us as already serene, confident and cheerful. He sees us not as pathetic victims of life, but masters of the art of living, not wanting sympathy, but imparting help to others, and therefore thinking less and less of ourselves, and full, not of self-concern, but of love and laughter and a desire to serve.

This is not just silly, wishful thinking, or an attempt to boost people up. Some have been cured of illness by holding before themselves constantly a new picture of themselves as cured and whole. Agnes Sanford tells of a small bedridden boy who longed to play football. Knowing his case—an important point—she told him to picture himself every day running at full speed down the football field. He was told to conclude his meditation with the words, "That's the way it's going to be!" In due time it was. He became whole. Let us accept that we have all been rather despicable creatures. But all that is past and forgiven. Let us look at the real selves which are in the making the moment we believe in their existence. We must recognise the possibility of change and believe in the self we are now in process of becoming. That old sense of unworthiness and failure must go. It is false and we are not to believe in what is false. If Christ thinks us worth dying for; if He believes—as He does—that He can make new men of us, we *must* believe it too and set it before us. We must see that as the true self, and keep in living touch with Him Who is at work on us already. His work on us is always healing and restoring.

We said (p. 27) that anxiety is caused frequently by a threat to our self-esteem. There is nothing that can strengthen and build up a true and justifiable self-esteem so powerfully as the thought that Another, Who is Himself all that we long to be, cares for us, and, so far from caring casually, for say an hour's interview, has committed himself to the task of making us like Himself however long it takes. This is one of the meanings of the Cross of Christ. He pledges Himself to go to the uttermost to redeem all men.

I found a lot of help in a pamphlet called *The Conquest of Nerves,* by W. D. Kendall. He writes thus:

> The acceptance of fear and superstition has produced that most fundamental mistake, the illusion of separateness, the error of imagining that we can be cut off from the Source of all inspiration, power and life, an error so devastating that it would scarcely be an exaggeration to attribute to it the sum total of human suffering and misery.
>
> An illustration may help us here—I want you to consider the principal difference between a pocket torch and an ordinary electric light. The torch is self-contained, having a battery of its own which sooner or later becomes exhausted and the torch useless. The electric light, on the other hand, is wired up to a power station from which it receives an unfailing supply of power. Apply this illustration. We habitually think of ourselves as being like the torch with a self-contained and definitely limited supply of vitality, intelligence and reserve of power, a supply which at any time, through causes over which we have no control, may become exhausted. The truth is quite other than this and salvation from our trouble is found in realising that man is always in touch with an inexhaustible Source of Inspiration and Power and Life.

I do not think that this changing the picture of oneself is just a silly trick. I think it is a matter of letting go our defeatist thoughts and realising that we belong to God, that He loves us and is longing to help us if we will only believe we can be changed and see the change beginning

already. Fifty times a day, if need be, we must throw out
the old picture that keeps coming back, saying inwardly
and with conviction, "I'm not like that now," and believing
that God, Who has already begun a changing work within
us, will not give it up, but that, if we will co-operate, He
can and will make us the men we want to be, sooner than
we ever imagined. "Weakness," "fear," "failure," "despondency"—these words no longer are true of us. They
are false. Let us not cling any longer to what is false, or
even argue with what is false. *Let us remove from false
images that attention which gives them life and power.* Calm
ability to live victoriously through every day as it comes,
knowing that God is with us and working within us, that
is the idea to which to hang on. We must bring it back if
need be again and again. That is the truth about us, and
the truth is mighty and prevails. "Believing a lie does not
make it true; it only makes it *seem* true. As we turn away
from our fears, they will one by one fade out of our lives."
Says Basil King in *The Conquest of Fear*,[1] "In proportion
as I ceased to show fear, the Life Principle hastened to my
aid. . . . The Life Principle having through unknown
millions of years developed the conquest-principle by meeting difficulties and overcoming them, the difficulties had a
value. . . . To me it seems basic to the getting rid of fear to
know that our trials, of whatever nature, are not motiveless."

Old fears have been lived with so long that they rush
back along their grooves very quickly and easily. A word
in a book or paper, or spoken by another, can touch off a
terrifying descent of naked fear. But if, quietly and with
determination, we re-establish the new, calm, confident
picture at which Christ is working, we shall win. It is
very hard to be buses when we have been trams for so long,
but if we fill up the tram-lines, we shall manage it!

[1] Basil King, *The Conquest of Fear*, pp. 24-5 (Doubleday, New York, 1953).

I heard of a tram-car that broke away from the tram-lines and rushed down a steep hill, and I know from experience that our fears, long harboured, can gather strength and power, and rush us down to a veritable hell of despondency. But we *know* the freedom and joy of being buses, held no longer in the grip of tram-lines, and by switching off that degree of attention which gives our fears their power, and holding steadily in front of us the true picture of ourselves, we can achieve freedom. If we do this often enough, we shall replace the habit of falling a victim to fear by the habit of winning, with all the grand feelings that go with winning some inner struggle. Often we shall have to do something definite and objective like calling on a friend and NOT telling him our symptoms, writing to a friend, going to the cinema, getting into the company of others, especially the young, so that environmental factors help us stop the tram. "When I am assailed with heavy tribulations," said Martin Luther, "I rush out among my pigs rather than remain alone by myself. . . . The human heart, unless it be occupied with some employment, leaves space for the devil, who wriggles himself in and brings with him a whole host of evil thoughts, temptations and tribulations which grind out the heart."[1] At all costs we are to retain the new picture of the new self and believe in it. We must believe in the self we want to become, and *act as though we were that already*. That belief makes the real self strong. As we go on and win little battles over the desire to yield to depression, to run away, to recite symptoms, to indulge in self-pity, to tout for the pity of others, to ask our doctor for a holiday recommendation, to lie down in despair; to brood over the fear of becoming ill or losing our job or losing the approval of someone or other or of God, the fear of losing prestige or of falling off

[1] Martin Luther, *Table Talk* (Hazlitt's translation, 1564). I owe the quotation to Dr. John Baillie, *A Diary of Readings* (No. 185, O.U.P.).

some pedestal, then the new picture will be etched more and more deeply and the new self will gather power, and we shall enjoy that sense of power immensely. We shall be transformed by the renewing of our minds. We shall begin to feel master of the situation and that will be wine to us. So far from fearing "loss of face" we shall accept ourselves as forgiven sinners whom God loves and who have no "face" to save. We can even do without the approval of others if we have God's approval. Sickly neurosis will fall away and the real self will emerge. It is worth a lot to win through to courage. Changing the position of the furniture and pictures in one's room helps to mark the new change one has made in one's picture of oneself. "I am not now the sick neurotic who used to sit *there* and mournfully brood and look into the fire. Now I am a different person, so I sit here and look at *others* through the window!" We must never forget that at every turn old habits of thought, old ways of looking at ourselves will try to trip us up with offers of sympathy. (Poor chap, he would do this and that, but he is ill.) But we must not sell courage to buy sympathy. It is like a skylark selling its wing feathers to buy worms. If the bird *worked* for worms, it would still be able to fly.

It is better to endure the tension and the torment of longing to run away and escape, than to lose self-respect and dodge duty. Cowardice costs too much in terms of depression and self-hate. We have often tried the cowardly way and known that it is hell paying for it. Courage is so very hard, but afterwards it pays a tremendous and most satisfying dividend. We must believe in the worthwhileness of the new person we are already becoming, and keep on looking at the picture of ourselves that Christ sees, believes in and is in process of creating within us.

Sometimes our picture of ourselves is of one who has been wronged or slighted or misunderstood. If so, it is important to realise that if we continually blame another, we shall lose the sense of being captains of our own souls, and that is bad and even dangerous. "I am the poor thing I am," we argue, "because I was treated thus by so and so." Even if that were true, nothing has happened to us that has not happened to others. The question is, "What are *we* doing about it? What are *we* making out of it?" *What matters most is not what happens to us, but our reaction to what happens to us.* The fact is that we *can* bear misunderstanding, abuse and anything that man or woman can do to us, and the self must not be allowed to wriggle out of facing life by retreating into illness. Even nervous tension can be borne, and the bearing turned into courage and ability to help others. Christ is stronger than we can ever imagine, but we must pay part of the price of the manhood He can confer, by refusing to lie down under strain.

Whatever we do, we must not cherish resentment. The man who does that is wrong with God and is divided within himself, for with half his mind he wants God to forgive him and with the other he will not forgive another. Jesus spoke about this as strongly as about anything. "Forgive us our trespasses *as we also have forgiven those who trespass against us.*"[1] And again, "If, therefore, thou art offering thy gift at the altar, and there rememberest that thy brother hath aught against thee, leave there thy gift before the altar, and go thy way, first be reconciled to thy brother, and then come and offer thy gift."[2] "To be reconciled with God," says my friend, Dr. James Stewart, "is to see all mankind with new eyes. It is to have the living Christ within, which means to feel towards others as Christ would feel towards them."[3]

[1] Matthew 6. 12.

[2] Matthew 5. 23.

[3] *A Man in Christ*, p. 226 (Hodder & Stoughton).

It is interesting to notice how St. Paul himself changed his picture of himself. Here is what he says about himself:

> In me (that is, in my flesh) no good dwells, I know; the wish is there, but not the power of doing what is right. I cannot be good as I want to be, and I do wrong against my wishes. Well, if I act against my wishes, it is not I who do the deed, but sin that dwells within me. So this is my experience of the Law: I want to do what is right, but wrong is all I can manage; I cordially agree with God's law, so far as my inner self is concerned, but then I find quite another law in my members which conflicts with the law of my mind and makes me a prisoner to sin's law that resides in my members. (Thus, left to myself, I serve the law of God with my mind, but with my flesh I serve the law of sin.) Miserable wretch that I am! Who will rescue me from this body of death? God will! Thanks be to Him through Jesus Christ our Lord![1]

And he seems to get the new picture by what he calls "putting on Christ," as if it were a matter of putting on a robe. Listen! "Put ye on the Lord Jesus Christ."[2] "Put on the new man."[3] "Ye have put off the old man with his doings and have put on the new man."[4] We too must thrust away our old pictures of ourselves as though to say, "Yes, I used to be like that, but now I'm different! The old self is 'dead.'" So Paul says, "Reckon ye also yourselves to be dead unto sin, but alive unto God in Christ Jesus."[5] And again, "Ye died and your life now is bound

[1] Romans 7. 18–25 (Moffatt's trans.).
[2] Romans 13. 14.
[3] Ephesians. 4 24.
[4] Colossians 3. 9–10.
[5] Romans 6. 11.

up with Christ in God."[1]   Dr. Maltby used to add, "And don't walk about after your own funeral.   It isn't done!"

Every Christian believes that Jesus Christ can change men's lives.   When does the change begin?   Isn't the answer, the moment we believe it can happen; the moment we alter the mental picture we have of ourselves?   Clean the slate of the mind of that old picture of a frightened, defeated, symptom-obsessed person; for Christ has a different picture in His mind.   It is that of a person serene, joyous, confident and victorious.

We can change the picture at once, and we should put this book down and begin now.   When the prodigal came home, over all his filthy, stained raiment was thrown the robe of sonship, symbol of the renewed relationship, the robe that made him look quite different.   Everybody on the farm saw the *son*, not the runaway.   He looked different to himself.   Though only yesterday he was with the swine and eating their food, today he is a son.   The picture of himself is different.

For instance, if emotionally a man is still a little boy of seven, who was afraid of the disapproval of Mummy and so tried always to placate her and "suck up" to her, so as to divert her anger; if he still treats similarly anyone in authority whose goodwill is desired, including God, then at once let him part from that picture of himself as a frightened, crawling, timid child.   Let him tear up that false picture.   Christ can make him a man.

Let us never again even look at ourselves wearing the rags of fearfulness, of self-despising, of inescapable failure, or of unconquerable sin.   If any man be robed in the new character Christ can give him, a new creation has begun already.[2]

We spoil our picture of ourselves by doing wrong, and

[1] Colossians 3. 3.

[2] cf. II Corinthians 5, 17 (R.V. margin).

then we cannot live with the picture we have made of ourselves as "wrong'uns." This inability spells insecurity and fear. A good conscience is the best security. If we are right with God, we can face life. If, by sin, we undermine our security and self-esteem, we try to bluff ourselves and hide our conscience-distress by blaming others. Indeed, any psychologist who hears a patient *constantly* blaming another is usually justified in the guess that the patient is repressing his own sense of guilt. When a man feels secure in the love of God, he is notably forgiving and tolerant of others. Our criticism of others, especially those who seem hindrances or rivals, is frequently a projection of our dissatisfaction with ourselves.

One of the inevitable things about life is that we have got to live with ourselves. What a misery it is to live with a person you despise, a person who has allowed fear to defeat him—even if it is yourself! And unaided we cannot help despising ourselves, the more we know ourselves! It is a new self made different through Christ that we need, and we can live with that new self because Christ, not we ourselves, has made him. Many people are always searching for the approval of others to counteract their disapproval of themselves. They must see themselves "in Christ." We can be independent of the approval of others only when we approve of ourselves, and we can only approve of ourselves if we have God's approval. We can do without men's approval when we are SURE we are worth something to Christ.

"Thou, O CHRIST, art all I want."

It is so hard for us to free ourselves from the prison of time, but God sees what He is going to make of us. We look at the daub and despise it. He looks into what we call the future and sees the picture after He has finished it.

c

That is why He is more concerned with our direction than our achievement. He is hindered if we turn back, but He rejoices when we think again, and start once more along the only road that leads us home. He can do anything with a man who is "going His way."

A friend of mine once told me a lovely story. He said that when he was a little boy, he was out for a walk with his father and they saw a most vivid rainbow, the end of which lit up the rocks quite near the path along which they were walking. The little boy said to his father, "Daddy, let me go and stand in the light of the rainbow," and off he went. But, of course, to the boy the light of the rainbow was always a little bit further on and never seemed to bathe him in its splendour. But when his father looked at his son, the glory of the rainbow light seemed to transfigure him. When we set ourselves to leave the paths of selfishness along which we have been walking, and seek to enter into spiritual realities, the light of the glory of God seldom seems to be round about us. It always seems a little further on. Sometimes we grow disheartened and depressed. Achievement falls so short of desire. But I think when our heavenly Father looks upon us, He sees the light of spiritual beauty around us because the glory of Christ transfigures a man immediately he steps off the path of selfish desire and longs to be caught up into the light and life of God. You may not discern the light around you, but God sees it and, more often than we think, other people do too.

I can think of many of my friends who carry with them a terribly distorted picture of themselves. They have no opinion at all of themselves, but I, who have known some of my people for twenty years, know that God is busy with them, making of them wonderful personalities for His glory and their eternal bliss.

VI

CONFESSION IS GOOD FOR THE SOUL

THERE is a passage in the letter of St. James, our Lord's brother, which few of us have ever taken very seriously. It runs thus: "Confess, therefore, your sins one to another . . . that ye may be healed."

I think we should begin this chapter by paying a tribute to that branch of the Christian Church which has always practised confession. I cannot myself wholly support the way in which Roman Catholics interpret this New Testament exhortation, for they make confession obligatory instead of voluntary, and they make it habitual when, in my opinion, it should be occasional. These two demands make it sometimes a substitute for sincere penitence instead of an expression of it. Further, they demand confession to a priest, whereas I am convinced that in many situations the professional ecclesiastic is not a suitable person to hear a confession. St. James clearly says, "Confess your sins *one to another*," and I should vote for the penitent's right to choose his confessor. In many cases, no one could be more suitable or efficient than some saintly, motherly woman, especially where the penitent is a young girl.

I should like to extend the scope of the subject to include not only sins, but sorrows, worries, doubts, fears and frustrations. In fact, anything that weighs upon the heart.

How wonderfully Shakespeare, who knew so much about the human heart, understood the value of pouring out to another that which weighs us down. In *Macbeth* we read:

Canst thou not minister to a mind diseased,
Pluck from the memory a rooted sorrow,
Raze out the written troubles of the brain,
And with some sweet oblivious antidote
Cleanse the stuffed bosom of that perilous stuff
Which weighs upon the heart?

In *Macbeth*[1] the answer of the doctor is an evasion, for he says:

"Therein the patient must minister to himself."

But that is so often what he cannot do. Another person is necessary for us adequately to exteriorise our troubles by giving them words. In another part of *Macbeth*, Shakespeare says:

Give sorrow words: the grief that does not speak
Whispers the o'er-fraught heart and bids it break.[2]

To my mind, John Wesley's emphasis on the priesthood of all believers is relevant to this matter of confession. There is no need to choose a priest or a minister. All true Christians are in a sense priests. Certainly it is convenient, since the ministry is so demanding, to have some men trained and set free from business worry, so that they can give their whole time to the specialised work of the ministry. But any true Christian has as much right to declare the forgiveness of God to a penitent, or explain the love of God to the broken-hearted, as has the priest. After all, it is not the priest who forgives, and the Anglican Church puts the matter clearly in the famous words: "*He* pardoneth and absolveth all them that truly repent." Anyone has the right to declare that *He* pardoneth.

[1] Act v. Sc. 3.
[2] Act iv. Sc. 3.

One objection will quickly leap to the mind, "Is it not sufficient to confess to God?" To which the answer clearly seems to be, "Yes, quite sufficient, as long as God is real," but so many people complain, in regard to their prayers, that they feel as though they are talking to nothing. If that is true, then the prayer of confession will not have enough feeling about it to make it cathartic. The man who prays will feel frustrated. It is a poor game trying to feel forgiven.

For this reason I recommend what I have practised myself many times. Confess, or pour out your troubles, to a carefully chosen friend. The neurotic tends to tell his story of trouble to anyone who will listen, but in order that he need not feel a compulsion to do this, it would be so much better if he had one, or perhaps two father confessors to whom he could go in absolute confidence. I am sure that in the Free Churches our people should be encouraged to find everything that is of value in this practice. Of course, confessors must have certain qualities, and I would suggest to them four "don'ts" which they should observe.

1. Do not interrupt unless you do not understand what is being said to you and wish to get the story clear in your own mind. Remember that a person coming to reveal his inner troubles often comes after much self-questioning and in a highly emotional state. A rough interruption, even if it is well intended, may be enough to put him off. Certainly we must not intrude our own experiences in the middle of his story because at the moment he is interested only in himself and feels that anyone else's troubles are a rejection on our part of his own.

2. Do not be shocked. To be shocked and to show that one is shocked is a self-revelation, paralysing to the listener, for it means that we are either ignorant of life, or else that we are pretending that life is what it is not. Even the half-concealed indrawing of the breath when a person

says a rather startling thing, may make him think, "O dear, now I've shocked him," and it may end his confidence and his confession.

3. Do not rebuke. The very fact that the person has come to you to confess his troubles means that he is clearly aware of the situation. To rebuke is to widen the gulf between you and the person seeking your help, and probably to make it so wide that the latter seeks only to end the interview. When fellowship has been established and our opinion is asked, we may say what we think about another person's conduct. But let us remember that our Lord did not rebuke even an adulteress, not because He was indifferent or complacent about adultery, but because the adulteress had already rebuked herself. Her attitude showed that clearly. If Christ had rebuked her, He would have broken something within her. Perhaps there is never any need to reproach another person, or rebuke him, unless he has so brazenly hardened himself that he cannot perceive that wrong has been done. But such a situation does not arise in the kind of case we are discussing, or the person concerned would not seek an interview.

4. Do not betray a confidence. This the hardest "don't" to observe, and frankly very, very few people can do it. Perhaps they tell their wives, or they tell another person, prefacing the revelation with, "Now I know you won't tell anybody, but . . ." or, "I am telling you in the greatest confidence, but . . ." and frequently the hearer proceeds to spread the story with the same preliminaries.

We can render enormous help to one another by using this machinery of the confessional. I remember a book, written twenty-five years ago in America, called *A Mind that Found Itself*, in which the writer, Mr. C. W. Beers, tells a tragic story of the way in which he imagined that epilepsy was infectious. His brother developed epilepsy, and the author of the book tells us that he got it into his head that he had fits himself, but that they happened in his sleep and were concealed from him by his parents.   In the end he threw himself out of an upper window in an unsuccessful attempt at self-destruction.   Fortunately he was not killed and found out the truth.   The tragedy is that one sentence from any friend in whom Beers had confided would have saved him ten years of mental anguish.

My reason for including this chapter is that there may be some reader with some haunting fear which he is keeping to himself and which makes him utterly miserable, and which could be driven out of his mind by a single conversation with an adequate person.   I have talked to people who thought that secret masturbation would bring an incurable disease, or rob them of their sanity.   I have talked to people who thought they had committed the unpardonable sin, whereas if you even think you have committed the unpardonable sin, it is evidence that you could not have done so.[1]   Sometimes people are victims of fears which would be laughable, save for the misery they cause to those who hold them.   Confess, therefore, your sins and worries and doubts and fears and frustrations to another that you may be healed.

What good does such confession do?

1. First of all, it cleanses the mind.   In a psychological and spiritual sense it does what a cathartic does to the body.   It clears out from the mind and the soul those things which, if left there, can poison personality.   Aristotle would explain to us, if we listened to him, that therein lies part of the value of the drama.   There are certain emotions which in polite society we cannot ourselves

---

[1] I have discussed "The Unpardonable Sin" in *When the Lamp Flickers*, Chapter 4. (Hodder & Stoughton).

express. We should like to express them, but we must not do so. When we see them expressed on the stage, we vicariously feel relieved by them. When you next go to the theatre, try an experiment during some exciting play which, I fear, will make you very unpopular if you repeat it often. At some tense moment in the drama, turn round and look at the faces of the people behind you. You will see reflected in their faces the emotions that are being expressed on the stage. If on the stage a man is murdering his mother-in-law and you turn round, you will probably see some man almost delirious with joy. He is undergoing a wonderful catharsis. Of course, I am not making a cheap gibe at mothers-in-law, for many of them are the salt of the earth, but I have made the point. Emotion, capable, if bottled up, of setting up resentment or anxiety, is expressed. When its energy is discharged, we feel better.

2. Confession relieves the conscience. We may very truly say, "Surely I can confide secretly in God and not risk publicity by telling another human being." I say again that if God is real, you can do just that. But how many people say to one, "I pray for forgiveness, but I don't feel that anything has happened"? Exactly! Now the strenuous demand and discipline of telling another human being our secret sins is fraught with such feeling that we do obtain this catharsis of which I have spoken. By doing this we get that emotional release that liberates us from prison. The measure of the demand made is the measure of the liberation won.

I would urge you not to imagine in regard to some sin, or fear, or sorrow, that you will "get over it." Of course, you will get over it in a sense. I know a woman who came to this country from abroad and on the voyage home she fell and broke her elbow. Instead of having it properly set, she "got over it," and now she cannot use her arm. If you get salt in your eye, you will get over it because the waters of the eye can dissolve salt, but if you get grit in your eye, you will not get over it because grit is not soluble in tears. If a man gets a piece of shrapnel into his lung and the shrapnel happens to be clean, the lung can deal with it. It may be that a little bit of the lung is no longer used, but the body wraps the shrapnel fragment in tissue and no permanent disability worth mentioning seems to occur. But if the shrapnel has dirt on it, then it is likely that pus and inflammation will be set up and the shrapnel will have to be removed. In a similar way, if the mind has some shock, such as bereavement, and the wound is treated with the antiseptic of faith in God's love and purposes, then all may be well. But if resentment against God, or the doctor, or the nurse, or someone else is buried in the wound, it will set up trouble later. Now guilt is just the kind of emotion which surrounds so many of the wounds the mind and soul have had to sustain. Modern psychological research shows again and again that guilt buried deeply in the mind can set up not only emotional, but even physical, distress.

I must not digress here to work this theme out fully, and indeed have done so elsewhere,[1] but I would emphasise the point that there are many people ill in mind and ill in body, who would never have fallen ill if they had confessed some sin, or series of sins, to any adequate Christian, who, in declaring the loving forgiveness of God, could have cleansed the wound which the soul sustained. The forgiveness of God is, in my opinion, the most powerful therapeutic idea in the world, and he who really experiences a sense of forgiveness does not realise what he has been saved from because he has been saved from it. He is like a

[1] See *Psychology, Religion and Healing*, pp. 320–47 (4th Ed., Hodder & Stoughton, 1954).

man pulled off a railway line in front of the express train. He does not realise what he has been saved from because he has been saved from it.

While we are talking about the value of confession in a case of guilt, it is worth remembering that often people suffer from exaggerated guilt. They feel abnormally guilty about a comparatively trifling thing. Many men and women lash themselves, for example, because sex thoughts come to their minds and they think that such thoughts prove that they are impure. In fact, of course, it only proves that they are normal, and though they may be sexually hungry, to be hungry is not a sin. If I steal a loaf because I am hungry, that is a sin, and if I steal a sexual experience involving another, that is a sin, a sin against God and the other and against my own self-respect; but in neither case is hunger to be called sin. Some people think that sexual self-relief is a terrible sin. If the imaginative picture on the screen of the mind at the time is one which we should be ashamed to show to Christ, then we must take some steps in the matter. But if the screen of the mind is empty, or filled only with the image of some person with whom we could legitimately have sex experience—such as the soldier away at war dreaming of his own wife at home—then it is not so much sin as an unsatisfactory habit; unsatisfactory because it is not a complete experience of love. Masturbation is often an expression on an immature level of self-love, and the long continuance of the habit may "fixate" sex at that immature level, but a burden of guilt should not be attached to it. It is strange that so many people harass their minds about trifles, and fail to see that a loss of temper, hypocrisy, cruelty to a child, intolerance of another through pride, are, in the New Testament assessment, much worse sins than are any of those linked with the sex instinct.

Confession to a wise person who is himself emotionally adult and experienced in the Christian life would get our sense of guilt into a right proportion. I remember reading of one woman who threw into the fire a piece of embroidery she had done most carefully, because the design was one of grapes. It suddenly occurred to her that wine was made from grapes, and that over-excess in wine made men drunk. She argued, foolishly enough, that the grapes might tempt some poor soul to resort to wine. The story sounds fantastic, but it happened, and again and again one has found people making themselves miserable through exaggerated guilt.

3. Confession ends the loneliness of pretence. It must have occurred to every reader that very often people live behind a façade. They wish to be taken for what they know in secret they are not. I cannot exaggerate to you the healthiness of following advice which is often colloquially put thus: "Come off it!" To sit down with some wise Christian adviser and to shed all pomposity and pretence, *to talk oneself out with a person*, to realise how foolish one is to pretend, is so very healthy. I recall a woman who said to a psychologist friend of mine, "The happiest day of my life was the day when I stopped trying to look twenty years younger than I am."

Even husbands and wives can live behind façades, and if their self-esteem is undermined, then one or the other will resort to a proud silence or a sulky mood. Sulking, of course, is the compromise-tension we set up through wishing to hit back and fearing to do so, but again and again sulking is the façade behind which hides a frightened and hurt baby—a baby all the more pathetic because he or she may be fifty or sixty years old.

I was privileged to read in the magazine published by Alcoholics Anonymous,[1] the story of a man who writes thus about his anxiety:

[1] April 1955, Vol. II, No. 11, p. 11 ff.

"The besetting torture of my life has been a sense of being in the wrong and liable to excoriation and punishment for it. Man and boy, I have tried many ways of dealing with this mental plague. I have tried bluster, proclaiming that I was not in the wrong at all, and wishful thinking, pretending the haunting feeling wasn't really there. I've tried stern repression, resolving not to let my mind dwell morbidly upon it, firmly turning my thoughts to more pleasant things. I've tried hard work, the pursuit of amusement and diversion, and God knows I've tried getting drunk. And regardless of my evasive manœuvres, there—when the chase was ended—it was, ready to pounce.

It is hard for me to describe the terror that goes with this sense of having been in error. I am almost physically allergic to the word "wrong" as applied to myself. I tense up and shorten my breath and feel scared at the mere mention of it. I go on the defensive at all points, fairly bristling, like a mental porcupine, yet with an underlying deeply panicked sense that my defence is not going to be successful. The word "wrong" directed personally to me, has all kinds of connotations, all of them unpleasant and some of them frightening. It means shouting, berating, scolding voices. It means threats of beatings and incarceration and ostracism and disgrace, an eternity of unfriendliness. It means ultimatums impossible to meet, standards that cannot be attained. My natural reaction is one of hate and fear and hostile defensiveness."

One night he was in such a state that he telephoned to two friends although it was very late, and asked them to help him. Their help consisted in listening to his painful recitation, but that night, he says, was "the real beginning of the deep personality change we all hope and pray for.

The kindness of God and man made it possible for me to admit wrong. When I could admit it, I was spared the exhausting effort of trying to maintain the façade of phony bluster and pretence intended to conceal wrong. I became less tense, more relaxed, less afraid of people, more willing to help them."

The experience made this man apply to others what he had found himself. He has talked with scores who have shared with him the deep things of the heart. He says that there are hundreds of people who could find relief if they would admit to God, themselves *and another person* that they had been wrong, and he tells us that although the experience is gruelling, the reward is a life lived fully and actively before God and man *completely without fear*. He says that he has to repeat the process, but that instead of the fearful retaliations of his morbid imagination, he experiences the kindness of God and of his friends which is so therapeutic that all his old phobias break up and vanish. He concludes his story with this sentence: "We cannot continue in the maintenance and growth of a spiritual experience until we can live with God, ourselves and man without the slightest fear of being found, from time to time, to be somewhat in the wrong, along with the rest of day-to-day humanity. The fear vanishes when we become ready to admit we're wrong, then go right ahead and admit it."

4. Finally, confession opens the door through which Christ comes. If we confess our sins and our worries, our fears, our doubts, our sorrows, our frustrations, our resentments, our bitterness, the evil things we have said to other people, and the anxieties that burden our minds . . . He is faithful and just to forgive us. He restores the relationship of love, trust and acceptance, as though we had never broken it. The Bible is full of that tremendous declaration.

The Biblical writers could not find language strong enough to tell us that if only we would, as it were, come clean with God—and confession to man is a way of doing just that—then our sins are put away as far as east is from west, as far as heaven is from earth. Worry flows out and trust flows in. Doubt is dispelled like a mist, and faith shines forth as the sun. For some people, anxiety could be ended by this simple process of confession. They would find uttermost love rushing in to redeem them.

Part of the message of the Cross is just this message of release from anxiety. Anxiety may sometimes be set up because we feel that we are in a situation in which we can do no more. But we are never in a situation in which God can do nothing. And often release from anxiety comes when, confessing all to Him, including that very anxiety, pouring it all out and admitting that we are beaten, we leave it to Him, only to find that indeed Christ can save to the uttermost them that come unto God through Him.

VII

THE DIFFICULTY OF FEELING
FORGIVEN

WHEN the victim of anxious fears gets his "down" days and the miserable symptoms described in Chapter 1 return, he often cannot get out of his head the idea that God is punishing him for sins, real or fancied, which were committed perhaps years earlier.

I think it would help such a victim first to ask himself whether part of his mind is tricking him; telling him that he deserves punishment and that his symptoms are that punishment. One of the commonest signs of an anxiety state is the delusion that what has happened is punishment, and that punishment is falsely attributed to God. When we realise that we are acceptable to God, "just as we are, without one plea," then, with clarified enthusiasm, we can go forward to change our pattern of living, so that never again will anxious fears cripple us. We can *feel* forgiven when we get a true idea of God and of ourselves.

It may be some help to such a person to read again the chapter about trusting God, and to realise that his mind may be still tied up with that old bogey of a god made frequently in the image of some tyrant of his youth, such as a dominating father or mother, or a sadistic schoolmaster. As a child he always connected feeling miserable with being out of harmony with that tyrant, his father, for example. So now, as soon as he feels ill and miserable, he feels out of harmony with his heavenly Father, for the two are inextricably associated and connected in his mind. He must reiterate one fact until it really possesses his mind, namely this:

GOD IS QUITE DIFFERENT.

Let me set down some other facts and ask the reader who needs them to try to receive them; not just intellectually, but feeling them and getting them into his ductless glands!

1. God completely understands us. He knows everything about us. Confession to Him is therefore not necessary from His point of view. From our point of view it is a good thing to confess our sins to Him because it helps us to "exteriorise our rottenness," as Dr. William James says, and avoid complacency. Confession can be a spiritual catharsis. Even for us, however, it is a bad thing to keep on confessing the same sin. Repeated confession of the same sinful happening makes it appear as if we have to *persuade* God to forgive us, as if He were a reluctant old tyrant, when really He is more ready and eager to forgive than we are to ask for forgiveness. Further, to keep on confessing the same incident means that our prayers can have a bad effect. They deepen the sense of failure and depression more than they give us a feeling of victory and release. The past, if repeatedly recalled, throws so heavy a shadow over the future that we cannot believe the sun will ever shine again. So we must hang on first of all to that point. God knows all we have done, both good and bad. He knows the way we have taken and everything that has contributed to our "make-up." To Him we are all lovable and worth an infinity of trouble. Jesus Christ revealed God's nature in every significant thing He did. No human being can go further, or do more, than give up his life. That represents his uttermost. Thus the Cross of Christ is the pledge that *God* will go to the uttermost for us and never wash His hands of us or leave us to perish.

2. This being so, He does not need explanations, let alone excuses. Assuming that we have made whatever restitution is possible, we do not need continually to run back mentally, as we sometimes do, recalling this case of moral failure and that person whom we perhaps cheated. Some of the people we wronged are dead, and we can be certain that they will not be bearing us a grudge, especially if they can see Him all the time. His pardon of *their* sins will stop them thinking twice of any wrong we may have done them. So we must not reminiscently think, "There was that time I failed in such and such a year. There were all those people I wronged when I was abroad. There was that wrong motive in what I tried to do to help so and so. . . ."

No, let us put all our sins and failures and mistakes in a big bag and, like Christian in Bunyan's masterpiece, put them all down at the foot of the Cross and say, "Lord, here they are and there are hundreds of things I've done and said and thought that hurt You, and I've never even seen them to be wrong, but I love You and I want to be Your man and serve and help You. You have already forgiven me. Now help me to accept complete release."

3. Then we must remember that forgiveness means *the complete restoration of a relationship*, and from God's side it is restored the moment we want it so. It is true that forgiveness does not stop all the consequences of our sins, for we live in a universe of cause and effect, but it changes them from being a kind of impersonal nemesis or soulless retribution, into becoming a friendly discipline that we must accept because God is using it and weaving it into His plan for us and others. Our *forgiven* sins can be qualifications enabling us to understand and help others. I do not mean that we have not lost something, but we have not lost all. And every man alive has lost *something*. All have sinned. All have come short. All will do so again. That

also must be accepted. The prodigal would never forget how he hurt his father and wasted his years and manhood, but when the relationship was restored, even though he took months to re-orientate and readjust, *he was at home* and in a love-relationship far better than the law-relationship which his elder brother thought was correct and all that could possibly be required of him.

4. When we come to God, He does not make us feel guilty with the kind of guilt that is full of terror and fear, because He is the loving Father, not the stern, threatening schoolmaster or tyrannical parent. He does show us that sin is in conflict with our best selves. He tries to show us, not so much that it does not pay, as that it does not work out for our real well-being. The road of sin does not bring us out where our best selves want to be. It ends in a blank wall. One has to turn back and find the right road. Getting lost does not mean being damned. It means not finding the way home. No one is lost who knows the way home. And God has so made life, and so made us, that there is only one way home, and that is His way, and by "home" I mean that state of mind in which we find the complete satisfaction of our highest selves. It is what the evangelists mean, and what the New Testament meant by "being saved." God knows us better than we know ourselves, and it must grieve Him to see us setting our hearts, with such energy and perseverance, on things like money and sex and fame and social advantages, that are much too trivial and transient to satisfy an eternal thing like the human soul. He says, "Come just as you are, not waiting to put your life in order or armed with twenty new resolutions, and in our new relationship I will show you"—says God—"the road that will take you towards your real goal, the one that will satisfy you. I made you for Myself and I am the only Satisfaction there is."

5. Then we may comfort ourselves by remembering that

the forgiven sinner can *go on*. That is so important. He has not got to keep chewing over past failures and sins. He is free now to move in the new direction and *he must move*. If he still allows the memory of past and forgiven sin to paralyse him, he is proving that he has not yet grasped the reality of Christ's forgiving love. He is behaving as though he had never heard of the Gospel. He is acting as though God through Christ had not acted. When things remind him of what a dirty dog he was—and they sometimes do this cruelly at three o'clock in the morning—he must say to himself, "Yes, I used to be like that, but I'm not now. I'm a forgiven sinner." The dirty dog is washed! Seriously, a forgiven sinner can trust his Father and *go on*, happily.

6. There is another point worth making. That horrid feeling of guilt is retained sometimes if in our hearts we are saying to God, "I want You and I want forgiveness; I want grace and I want to feel happy again—but I'm going to keep on this sin or that." I remember a married man getting into a wrong relationship with a woman, and although ill and miserable, he felt he could not give her up because to do so would be "letting her down." No wonder the poor fellow could not find release. He *had* apparently to "let her down," or else let his wife down and God down and his own soul down. Friendship is one thing, but an emotional entanglement involving sex excitement which cannot find expression without "sin" and lost self-respect ought to be broken, or everybody will be let down.

If we are honest with ourselves, we shall know at once if we are saying to God, "I'm Yours, but on *my* terms," or, "I want to be well, but on my terms. You must not enter into every room of my house of life." We shall know if those terms mean holding back from the full surrender of *all* of our nature and affairs to His will as far as we can see it at that moment. He demands that all be offered and nothing held back. But our surrender spells our peace of mind. We feel, then, that we really are forgiven, and frequently there surges into the heart such a sense of liberty and release that we are set free even from our morbid fears. Physical health has, again and again, been found in over-flowing measure when the forgiveness of God has been really accepted.

7. There is only one other point perhaps worth making. If we still feel unable to take God's forgiveness, may not our inability sometimes be a queer bit of pride? Are we, in spite of the evidence of our known sins, saying in our hearts, "I'm not really the kind of man these sins would suggest. I'm not as bad as many others. In fact, I'm not a bad chap really"? Do we still pretend, even with Him?

I think it is when we really believe that we are sinners; when we really recognise that we cannot pretend any more, that we have done, or at any rate thought, things for which other men, after exposure, have been shamed and ruined; when we realise that we cannot buy, earn, merit or begin to deserve forgiveness, that we sink down and cry:

> "Nothing in my hand I bring,
> Simply to Thy Cross I cling."

Then, at last, without a shred of respectability or excuse left, we find that a great tide of love and pity and mercy flows out to us, and we begin for the first time to feel forgiven and able to see the slate wiped clean before our very eyes. Then the weighty burden of sin really falls off, leaving us *free to go on* unhampered in a true direction along the pathway of His will for us. We feel that even though men knew what rotters we were, even if we were shamed and rebuked by men, He would still believe in us and love us and pick us up and accept us and send us joyfully along His road for us.

A friend once said to me, "When a man slips and falls in the street, he does not stay there. He rises, kicks into the gutter the fruit-skin which made him fall, *and then he goes on*."

As Bunyan said in *The Pilgrim's Progress*, "So I saw in my dream that just as Christian came up with the Cross, his burden loosed from off his shoulders, and fell from off his back and began to tumble, and so continued to do, till it came to the mouth of the sepulchre, where it fell in, *and I saw it no more*. Then was Christian glad and lightsome, and said, with a merry heart, 'He has given me rest by His sorrow and life by His death.'"

VIII

NOT TO WORRY

I HAVE adopted the above title because it is a phrase often used by a dear friend of mine, but we must be careful not to become the kind of superior person—or supposedly superior—who pats another heartily on the shoulder and, having nothing to worry about himself, says, "Not to worry," or, "Now don't worry, don't worry!" It is useless advice, and it irritates by its patronising superiority. It is better to try to understand what worry is and whether we can take any steps to exorcise that fear-created devil.

First of all, I separate worry from concern. My wife says that when she is concerned I call hers "worry," and when I worry I tell her that my feeling is only concern! But if she is out in the evening and has said she will be in by nine o'clock and has not returned by ten, or even eleven, of course I am troubled. If I were not, all it would prove would be that I did not care. But I call that "concern." It is a sign of love. What real husband would be content to sit by the fire thinking, "I don't know where she is," with the implication, "I couldn't care less"? That *concern* would prompt me to telephone to some of her friends on whom she might have called, or to the place where the meeting which she had attended was held, or to the garage where she leaves the car. If the word "worry" *must* be used, it is legitimate worry and makes me *do* anything I can to ease the situation.

I would reserve the word "worry" for that fruitless activity of the mind which keeps thoughts revolving endlessly without issue in action. It is like racing a motor-car engine without letting in the clutch. One wastes petrol and energy, but one does not move. Worry exhausts one and yet one does not move through one's problem.

That brings me to the first practical thing we can *do*, and that is to make sure what we are worrying about. That may sound a silly thing to say, but I am sure it is good advice. I would counsel a person not to "try to put it out of his mind," as some people advise, at least not yet, but rather to set it right in the centre of his mind and look at it in isolation, making sure that he knows every detail and facet of the worrying situation. Writing out the whole thing is often of value. Suppose, for example, I am worrying that so-and-so will try to blackmail me, or report me, or that I am worrying about whether I shall lose my job or my health, or that I am worrying about whether I have got cancer, or have no security for my old age, and so on, I must calmly set the whole situation out and try to look at it in isolation from other problems.

This isolation prevents the mental distress from spreading through the mind in which case one rapidly worries about *everything*, and becomes irritable and harder to live with. It is possible to lose sight of, and actually "forget," the origin of the worry, but it is there, functioning deep in the mind and sending up to conscious life all sorts of vague fears and fancies and even physical symptoms. By isolating it in consciousness and confronting it steadily, we *may* find that we are worrying about something that is most unlikely to happen, or some situation with which, with God's help, we can deal adequately and perhaps quite quickly.

The second practical thing is to say, "Right! So I'm worrying about that. Now what can I DO?" Doing is like letting in the clutch that makes the hitherto uselessly racing engine carry one forward through the difficulty. Often I have lain awake worrying how to answer some difficult letter, and then it has dawned on me that it is far better to sit up in bed and write it out, however roughly, and then sleep! So, if we can DO something, let it be done at once! If not, can we *decide* what to do? Deciding is a kind of doing. We may decide, for instance, to get a first-class physician to overhaul us. That will end the worry about whether we have got some disease or not. Sometimes we cannot even get as far as that, but perhaps we can say—"If this happens, I will do that. If that happens, I will do this."

One other word about doing. I was saved from a bad mistake by a friend who reminded me of what I ought never to have forgotten. "Never make a big decision," he said, "when you are depressed." A long winter, a spell of illness, lack of sunshine and fellowship, prolonged concern for the health or well-being of a loved one, and we can get "low" and, in panic, make decisions which we afterwards regret.

My own third step is to ask and answer this question, "What, in regard to this worrying situation, is the very worst that could happen?" "Come on, men!" Donald Hankey used to say when he led his men against the enemy in the First World War, "If you're hit, it's Blighty. If you're killed, it's the Resurrection." When we have looked steadily at the worst that could possibly happen, then what is *likely* to happen often seems quite mild! For when we look at the worst, we go on to realise how we would meet that worst, what aid we would summon, what inward resources we would call out, what friends would help us with advice, care, and even financial aid. It is not silly to say, "Well, if the worst comes to the worst, I'll do this." It is the highest wisdom. Said Lin Yutang, the Chinese philosopher, "True peace of mind comes from accepting the worst."

Let us remember too, how frequently we worry about a matter that never develops at all. For myself, I can say that the things I dreaded most have never happened. What a parable there is for us all in the walk those women took towards the tomb on the first Easter morning! "They were saying amongst themselves, Who shall roll us away the stone from the door of the tomb? And *looking up*, they see that the stone is rolled back; for it was exceeding great."[1]

One thing is very clear; to fight worry, one just must not sit and brood. So when we have decided what we are worrying about, looked the thing right in the eye, done anything that can be done, or decided what to do in any of the eventualities we can foresee, including the unlikely worst, then we should try to forget the worry by a game of golf, or bird-watching, or a concert, or the cinema, or a theatre, or a long walk with a friend. The mind needs FUN as well as worship, laughter as well as rest, fellowship as well as lonely prayer.

I recently made one silly mistake when I had a big decision to make. I asked too many people their opinions. Some of them, through no fault of theirs, of course, did not know enough about it to advise. And I forgot one important thing; that when one is nervously tired or "worked up" about anything, one is more than ordinarily suggestible. So I would come home one evening, having talked it over with Mr. A, and say to my wife, "I am going to do this." The next night, having talked it over with Mr. B, I would say the opposite. I got sick of talking about it and arguing. Finally, a friend who knows me better than he knew the situation, said, "Have a bash at it!" I decided to do so and only found peace by resolutely sticking to that decision and not listening to anyone else, feeling that, *whatever the consequences*, I now knew that that was the path I had to tread. A definite decision is of enormous help. It ends conflict and kills most of the fear in the state of anxiety. Further, it helps us to get things into a better proportion.

[1] Mark 16, 3.

Resolving a big worry by a decision makes little worries look silly. Women stop worrying about whether the house is clean, or whether a new hat suits them, when they have had to help their husbands to face a major operation. It is such a waste of energy to be worried by wondering if the sweep did the chimney properly, or whether it will rain on washing day, or whether Aunt Edith will drink out of her saucer when the vicar comes to tea.

In the matter of worry, there is enormous help for us in the Christian religion. I have not left it until last because it is unimportant, but rather to emphasise that there is a lot of religion in things that do not sound religious.

For myself, I do not think I could have got through without religion. It is perhaps the maximum help to remember that God is there, the Friend Who understands and sustains in every experience we have to face, and to Whom, in a real sense, we can hand over. He is the Lord of history, the Master of every "accident," the Weaver of a pattern that may have to be changed, but which He can still make beautiful and meaningful. We shall never be in the kind of situation Jesus was in on Good Friday morning, and yet God brought Him through with triumph, and wove a Cross that was caused by the plotting of evil men into a pattern which now we call "the redemption of the world through our Lord Jesus Christ." So our "crosses" may be thrust upon us by factors which are evil, but God can weave them into a pattern which we shall one day gladly and thankfully admit is good. "You meant evil against me," said Joseph to those who plotted his death, "but God meant it for good."[1] God can deal with every situation that makes us worry. He always knows a way through. To begin each day with a positive assertion that He can bring us through is perhaps the most important ingredient in our prescription for anxiety.

[1] Genesis 50, 20

I am sure that if we commit our way to Him, He will take responsibility for what happens. If only we could get that right into our ductless glands! We get so worried about what will happen if . . . We think of half a dozen things that might happen and, before we know where we are, our errant imaginations can get us wallowing in worry. Yet we really know that because He is our Father, understanding, loving, wise and finally omnipotent, His plans cannot go finally wrong. His purposes know no final defeat.

We worry ourselves into a panic by thinking we must achieve this or that, but God is saying to us, "Do your best day by day in what you honestly believe to be My will for you, and I will take care of the rest. I can use honest failure as powerfully as glamorous success."

I remember with what joy I discovered years ago this text, "In all thy ways acknowledge Him and He shall direct thy paths." To rest on that, is to find mental peace. To act on it, is to kill worry and banish anxiety.

IX

LIVING A DAY AT A TIME

THE kind of person for whom I am writing these chapters will find that he sometimes has dark days. So do I, and so do thousands, but, thank God, they do pass. Good days will outnumber them, and we must not neglect to use them. They are the days in which to rejoice, to give thanks to God, and to realise that even one good day means that final victory is certain. We can lay in spiritual provisions on the good days, and the bad will be conquered all the sooner. In the meantime, we must let the bad days just roll over us without getting too upset or "down" about them. We must not say, "I am as bad as I ever was." Remember the graph on page 26.

In this chapter I want to pass on a message that has often sustained me. It came home to me through those brave words of Robert Louis Stevenson who had so many dark days, namely that "every man can get through till nightfall." Tomorrow is another day. Let us not frighten ourselves today by looking at tomorrow and the day after tomorrow, let alone next month and next year. I have read that Sir William Osler, who became Regius Professor in the University of Oxford, attributed his success to following out a sentence he read as a young medical student. The sentence, written by Thomas Carlyle is as follows: "Our main business is not to see what lies dimly at a distance, but to do what lies clearly at hand." Sir William used to advise his students to "live in day-tight compartments." Similarly Viscount Grey, who as Foreign Secretary carried such a heavy burden during the First World War, wrote: "Looking forward to the months and years that are to come is very dreary and depressing, but we do not live life in the lump, but day by day, and each day brings its own work and some expedient to help us."[1]   I have frightened myself sometimes by wondering how on earth I was going to get through certain tasks lying months ahead.   And yet, faithless as I was, timid and with no confidence, somehow the Lord brought me through.   That sounds pious, but I mean it very sincerely and here is a personal example.   My church sent me on a four-month trip to America in the hope of raising money for the rebuilding fund of the City Temple in London.   I am not good at money-raising and I started off in fear of failure, of coming home, as I imagined myself doing, without having raised even my own expenses.   The voyage out was five days of misery and apprehension, and it would do no good to dwell on the increasing tiredness, from which I could never seem to gain relief.   Yet, the very first Sunday, enough money was given me to cover my expenses each way. When I fell ill, a doctor gave me a series of injections which enabled me to speak twice a day for five days to over a thousand people.   My elder son on one dark day motored three hundred miles and cheered me as only a loved one can. Later, he and his wife entertained me in their home.   Two friends gave up their summer holiday to motor me to various appointments, saving me the immense fatigue of train travelling.   My second son and his wife entertained me and allowed me to rest in their home, and I was able to fulfil nearly all my appointments in the far west.   To crown all, a millionaire, who became a real friend, gave me a tour manager, who also became my friend.   He arranged my hotel and aeroplane assignments and warded off reporters and attended to a hundred details.   The millionaire sent me home across the Atlantic with a gift for my church which

[1] G. M. Trevelyan, *Life of Viscount Grey of Fallodon*, p. 343.

was more generous than I ever dreamed of.   I ought never
to be depressed again.   Yet, even now, I have dark days
full of a sense of failure and sometimes I look into that black
pit that is called despair, and I know that thousands of
sensitive people do the same.

I am sure that the darkness is often physically caused.
I was comforted by some words I read in John Casteel's
fine book called *Rediscovering Prayer*.[1]

The phrase "dry times" has been used to describe
those states and seasons of prayer which seem devoid
of any sense of reality; or of any joy, or inspiration, or
renewal of courage, or without any consciousness of the
presence of God and His response to our praying.   The
mood, or inner condition, accompanying these states
may range from a mild sense of tedium, or an inner
enervation, to a state of interior turbulence or appre-
hensiveness which makes almost impossible, not only
prayer, but any kind of settled, purposive activity.

We do not know all the causes behind these states of
mind and spirit.   Physical fatigue, depletion of energies,
imbalances in glandular secretions, and other organic
factors have something to do with our spiritual vigour
and sensitivity.   Most of us have, unwittingly, trained
and conditioned our emotional responses so that from
time to time we fall into periods of lassitude, depression,
or moroseness—sometimes because such moods allow us
to indulge ourselves in the sweets of self-pity!   This
"psychosomatic" conditioning will assert itself in our
times of prayer, as it does in all our activity.

There is no doubt, also, that at that level of our mental
and emotional life which lies below full consciousness, a
continuing struggle goes on between our egocentric self
and the raw material of experience which it strives to

[1] Pp. 186–7 (Hodder & Stoughton, 1955).

exploit for its own ends. Our dreams rise out of that inner life, like oceanic islands on the peaks of submerged volcanic ranges; and the sense of exhaustion brought upon us by a particularly vivid and distressing dream should suggest to us that, waking or sleeping, we are having to supply the energies for this hidden life of the mind. We should expect, therefore, to find ourselves at times tired, distraught, unable to centre down into living prayer, although we cannot seem to give any clear reason for our fatigue.

And that kind of fatigue is so often a symptom of fear.

Some psychologists believe that fear can rise in the individual from the deep lake of mental life which, like an underground sea, joins all unconscious minds together; the "collective unconscious" as some call it. Others believe that a fear one's ancestors had from some specific events, a fire for instance, can rise in one's mind centuries later, as an exaggerated horror of fire. If these things are true, it is not much good going on indefinitely with a psychological analysis. But, however these fears may be caused, I have found help in a dark day by saying one or two things to myself.

One is that anyway all I have to do today is so-and-so, visit this hospital, dictate my letters, interview this person in trouble, chair this meeting, start my reading for such-and-such a sermon, and then, whatever it is, I try to concentrate my mind wholly on that one thing that I have to do at that moment. Anything is better than letting the mind brood over a situation that has not yet arisen.

The best thing about the future is that it is offered to us a day at a time. A friend of mine, Dr. Boreham of Australia, whom I got to know when I visited that country, told, in one of his books, of an occasion on which he was staying in a home for a few days, and noticed that written on one of the window-panes, as though with a diamond, were these words from one of the Psalms: "This is the day that the Lord hath made. Let us rejoice and be glad in it." When he went down to breakfast, he said to his hostess, "I am curious to know why that text is written on my window." She said, "I was going through great trouble and sorrow. When the morning came I wished it were evening, and when the evening came I wished it would all end. Then I did a thing that you will laugh at me for doing. I just let the Bible open of itself and the first words that took my eye, I received as a message from God. The message that met my eye was this: 'This is the day that the Lord hath made. Let us rejoice and be glad in it.' I thought to myself, 'That gives me a clue for my life.' I am worrying. I am brooding over the past. I am grumbling about the present. I am terrified of the future. I will just grasp the opportunity of this day and live out this day."

What a contrast we find in the New Testament compared with the Old in this matter! In the Old Testament the passing of the days brought one nearer a death which was gloomy and dark indeed. Hence the writers kept asking God for "many days" that they might postpone the dread day of death. The reward of virtue was repeatedly shown to be "many days." "What man is he that desireth life, and loveth many days, that he may see good? Let him keep his tongue from evil and his lips from speaking guile."[1] "Honour thy father and thy mother: that thy days may be long upon the land which the Lord thy God giveth thee."[2] "With long life will I satisfy him,"[3] and so on.

Yet Paul, while he revels in life, feels that to depart and be with Christ would be far, far better.[4] Paul was

[1] Psalm 34, 12–13.

[2] Exodus 20, 12.

[3] Psalm, 91, 16.

[4] Phi'ippians 1, 23.

not free from the symptoms lesser men often have. Listen to these sentences for there is comfort in them. Paul, who healed others, suffered both physically and mentally. He asks God repeatedly to remove his "thorn in the flesh."[1] The illness appears to me to have been some form of psycho-somatic disorder. It was certainly accompanied by anxiety, depression, fatigue and insomnia. He writes: "It was in weakness and fear and with great trembling that I visited you."[2] And again: "I was crushed (? depressed), crushed far more than I could stand, so much so that I despaired even of life."[3] And again: "I got no relief from the strain of things, even when I reached Macedonia; it was trouble at every turn, wrangling all round me, fears in my own mind."[4] Later, writing to the same community, he refers to his insomnia and tells them he passed many a sleepless night.[5]

I think those whose lives form the great biographies which inspire us, would support the message of this chapter. They would tell us to live a day at a time, sometimes an hour at a time. As the days pass, we may shut the door on them. They are over. We are travelling towards light and liberty, not towards darkness and fear. Tomorrow is a new day with a strength of its own. It is a good idea, often recommended, that each day we should tear off that page of the calendar that marks the day that is gone and mentally put that day away. Nothing can be altered. If it has been a good day, thank God. If a bad day, rejoice that it is over and you are neither in gaol nor in hospital! Tomorrow is another day. "As thy days so shall thy strength be." Since we cannot get tomorrow's strength

[1] II Corinthians 12, 7-9.
[2] I Corinthians 2. 3 (Moffatt).
[3] II Corinthians 1. 8 (Moffatt).
[4] II Corinthians 7. 5 (Moffatt).
[5] II Corinthians 11. 27 (Moffatt).

D

until tomorrow, how futile it is to try today to carry tomorrow's burden!   With the burden will come the strength
and the guidance.   Wasn't this what Jesus meant when He
said, "Don't fret about tomorrow.   Today's cares are
quite enough for today"?[1]   And let us not forget that He
also said, "I am with you all the days, even unto the end."[2]

By all means let us *plan* ahead, but let us *live* a day at a
time, thinking positively, looking with faith and trust at
God and committing ourselves wholly to Him Who loves,
understands, forgives, accepts and empowers.

> Every day is a fresh beginning;
>   Listen, my soul, to the glad refrain,
> And, spite of old sorrow and older sinning,
>   And puzzles forecasted, and possible pain,
>   Take heart with the day and begin again.

After all, did not Jesus teach us to pray, "Give us *this* day
our daily bread"?   And day by day He will give us all the
other things that we need.   No one knows better than He
that man does not live by bread alone.

[1] Matthew 6. 34.
[2] Matthew 28. 20.

X

THE AGE OF ANXIETY

WE hardly need W. H. Auden, the poet, to tell us that this age could well be called "The Age of Anxiety." We have only to look at the faces of our fellows in bus, or tube, or train—and probably they have only to look at ours—to see the indubitable evidences of nervous strain, and frequently the inward fear which so often accompanies it. Such fear, if life were easy-going, might have remained chained like Bunyan's lions, but nervous strain has worn the links of the chains so thin that first one and then another lion is liberated to bring fear into situations normally carefree. Where the spring lambs of joy should be gambolling in happy abandon in radiant sunshine, the sinister lions of fear move about in a perpetual winter twilight of fret and anxiety. Not yet do the lion and the lamb lie down together. We might call this the phenobarbitone age, though some people make aspirins do! I am informed that life in London largely limps along on luminal! One report says that in one year, 67 million sleeping tablets were prescribed in Britain under the National Health scheme. This was exclusive of the millions more purchased privately.

The causes of widespread anxiety are not far to seek, though it is not of such importance to stress the causes as to find the cure. The strain due to war is slowly working through many natures and finding physical expression for long pent-up fear. It is a well-known fact that if the mind is asked, over an indefinite period, to bottle up an emotion inimical to its well-being, it will compel the body to take over its burden in terms of physical malaise, especially where the latter relieves the former of at least part of its strain. A psychiatrist whom I met in America thinks that even until 1957 British people who endured the bombing will still be paying the price of war strain in terms of physical illness, and many a case of arthritis, asthma, gastric and duodenal ulcer, skin rash, coronary thrombosis and so on, though only now developing, can probably be put down to war strain. Thus, in many cases, we can account for the perpetual tiredness and the ailments which make a person admit that he "never really feels quite well," and from which so many suffer.

Another factor contributing to the anxiety of the age is noise, about which I could write much. For instance, investigation has shown that though a person may not be awakened by noise, its presence sets up muscular tension and strain even during his sleep, and produces in the body the very toxins of fatigue which rest would neutralise if quietness existed. One American investigator claims that if a man is sleeping in a bedroom past the windows of which a tram rattles from time to time, though the sleeper may not be awakened, he is subjected to as much muscular strain through unconscious tension every time the tram passes as would be produced by his holding a brick in his hand at arm's length for the same period.

Even in quiet country places where peace was wont to be found, noise now penetrates.

> "The silence that is in the starry sky,
>   The sleep that is amongst the lonely hills"

may now be shattered by the jet aeroplane. Soon there will be no area in these islands so secluded that a helicopter may not settle on one, or a visitor from Mars step out from behind a gorse bush!

Add to the noise the nightmare of moving about in traffic-jammed streets, strap-hanging in packed trains and buses, queueing whether for fun or food, and the hectic tempo of our daily life, and we are left with little energy to keep the lions of fear chained in the remote dungeons of the mind.

In a sentence, *there is too much going on*. Excitement, turmoil, rush and marvel infect even quiet homes. Speed is a demon worshipped by many. "Let's move fast" seems the unspoken slogan which directs thousands of restless people, some of whom are already planning interstellar travel.

If a mind had complete integrity and inward serenity, none of these factors could take its peace away. But when a mind feels—as most minds do—an inner sense of insecurity and vague anxiety, then these factors can be enough to produce all the symptoms I have described and rob us of happiness.

Science, which could contribute so wonderfully to man's welfare, sends to the table of the mind a new plateful of indigestible material before we have swallowed the last helping. The science of physics, though it has immensely widened our knowledge, has produced a greater degree of fear than of comfort. The science of psychology, to which men have hungrily turned, has proved that of itself it is impotent. Since more and more people continually consult the psychiatrist, it is important to see what psychology does and does not offer. It opens up the way in which the mind works, but that is not sufficient. Psychiatric treatment, in my view, has four stages, though sometimes, like prison sentences, they run concurrently, and I have made the treatment sound simpler than it often is. (1) The patient tells his story. (2) The patient, with the help of his psychiatrist, via the interpretation of his dreams and unconscious processes, and within the medium of the transference relationship between psychiatrist and patient, gains insight into his plight. (3) The patient emotionally re-lives earlier traumatic experiences which fixed his faulty behaviour pattern and sees the necessity of escaping the bondage of that pattern and reacting differently to life's pressures. (4) The patient begins to react to his circumstances in a new, creative and positive way based on his new insight.

Alas, it is at stage four that the patient so often falls down on the demands made on him. He "fears to launch away." He is slow to react in new ways. Old ways are like old friends who resent being deserted, and the older the patient, the greater the difficulty. So slowly do old dogs learn new tricks. With great difficulty does a tram get off its lines and become a bus, with all a bus's freedom. It is stage four which we must watch if we undergo psychiatric treatment. We must ACT on the new insights we have gained.

The science of medicine prolongs our lives until we wonder whether this is wholly a good thing. Many elderly people wish they were dead, and live in perpetual fear of becoming useless and burdensome, and of being allowed to feel so. Those who look after them must realise how sensitive they are.

As for political changes, we look to them in vain. As Studdert Kennedy wittily said, "At each election we take one lot of sinners out and put another lot of sinners in," but though we change the actors, the drama on the political stage continues, and the plot—one had almost said the plotting—remains the same. The spirit of restlessness reigns here also and so often political expediency replaces what should be sincere leadership towards a worthwhile goal. Overseas the restlessness appears to be even greater. One cannot, for example, keep up with the changing government of France. One knew at one o'clock, but one missed the six o'clock news!

Add to all this the vague threat of the possibility of a new world war, fought, it is too commonly imagined, with incredibly horrible weapons of atomic design, and one is not surprised at the increase of anxiety amongst us.

In the United States of America I am told that one in every twelve persons spends some period of his life in a mental hospital. In one state there are six hundred mental patients admitted to hospital each year, and in that great land of one hundred and sixty million people, over half a million can be found in its mental hospitals. In this country the figures are lower, but high enough to cause concern.

It is not surprising, then, that in the minds of a great many people there is a desire for escape coupled with the fear of being thought a quitter. Desire and fear in the same mind spell anxiety, and anxiety makes us want to run away. It is legitimate, of course, to escape temporarily to nature, to music, to art, to sport, to film, to drama and to hobbies, but unless these things lead further than themselves as, for example, nature and music and art can do, we must realise that they are anodynes for anxiety and not cures.

Some people would like to go back if they could to what they call simpler days. Mr. Gandhi made his followers burn machine-made fabrics and turn once more to the spinning-wheels of earlier days. But, alas, we cannot retreat into the past, nor would our problem of anxiety be solved if we could. Indeed, some people would fuss and fume as much about catching a stage-coach as an aeroplane, and though many of the factors which we have been considering contribute to anxiety, their absence does not guarantee peace of mind.

Religion ought to help and the Christian religion ought especially to help. Men feel that and wonder why it does not help more. Part of the truth is that religion is not magic, though men persistently wish it were and behave as though it were; praying, for example, that certain things should happen without any sincere attempt to provide the only conditions under which their prayer can be answered. We must not only pray to be free from anxiety, but try to understand and remove its cause. No man prays about his teeth. He goes to his dentist. Many a man would find that an hour's honest talk with a Christian psychiatrist would take him further than a month's prayer, just as twenty minutes on an operating table would do more for a patient suffering from, say, appendicitis, than a week of prayer. Prayer is of value in every situation, but it is not always of direct therapeutic value, nor is it always the greatest help that can be given. A great deal of unwise prayer, for example, increases our sense of guilt and yet gets us no further. Frequently the prayer of confession casts us into paralysing depression because forgiveness is not gladly accepted. Prayer is no cure-all. If it were, medical, psychological and other forms of research would become unnecessary. Further, the aim of praying is unity with God, and not merely the regaining of one's health. Prayer is degraded if, when medicine, surgery and psychology fail, we do what a man once described to me as "trying a spot of prayer."

But part of the reason why religion does not help us more is that there is too wide a gap between the religious truths we intellectually accept, and the truths by which we really live. It is one thing to sit in church singing hymns about trust and it is another thing really to live as though we *did* trust God. Real trust *does* challenge anxiety. I am afraid it is true to say that while there is such a wide gap between the truths men say they believe and the truths on which they rely, it can hardly matter much what religion a man professes. How many people do we know who really possess Christ's peace? How many of the thousands, who every Sunday sing hymns about trusting God, find that they have learned Christ's secret, and therefore that they never get in a panic, or what is commonly called a "flap," in the office, or in the home, even when things go wrong. Men who are honest realise that though they sing about peace, they have never worked hard enough on themselves to provide the only conditions under which peace of mind can be enjoyed. They have never discovered through their religion or elsewhere the experience about which a few people can speak with enthusiasm. Very humbly, therefore, let us bow before Christ and ask to be shown the way.

> "Thy secret tell; help me to bear
> The strain of toil, the fret of care."

It is clear that Christ did not find His inner peace from His environment. As a baby in His mother's arms no doubt He had the security which is every babe's birthright. But as a young Man, His mother and brothers clearly misunderstood Him. At one point they let it be known openly that they thought He was mad. When He called His twelve Apostles to be with Him, they were not nice, quiet people with whom it is easy to live. Two of them who sound to us gentle enough, were called "the sons of thunder." They all seem to have quarrelled for precedence. They all misunderstood Christ's purposes, and they all forsook Him when He needed them most. He died almost alone, His cause apparently defeated, His followers scattered, His body tortured, His mind, just before His death, in an agony of what felt like desertion. Yet perhaps in His last words He gave us a lifetime's secret: "Father, into Thy hands I commit My Spirit."

So, though serious anxiety may need the help of a psychiatrist because it springs from unconscious levels of the mind, for most of us there is real help in the Christian religion. Consider the following four factors:

1. Jesus looked away from Himself to God. Even in His anguish He did that, and called God "Father" at a time when it must have felt as though an omnipotent Father might have guided Him in a far less agonising path. In circumstances far less tragic, in the fret and turmoil of this age of anxiety, there must be continually for us times when we contemplate God, meditate upon Him and try to rest our fear-tossed minds in His greatness and adequacy. Was it not Emerson, rushing out of some committee meeting where argument and mental strife had raged, who, while he was still hot and hectic, heard the stars say to him, "Why so hot, little man?" How wonderfully the silent stars, in their majesty and remote beauty, hush our spirits, as if they were really saying, "God is great enough to take care of you," and, "Nothing troubling you is nearly as important as it seems."

Or again, when you turn your eyes from the vast heavens to the tiniest flower and really meditate upon it, you may find your anxiety hushed. Have you ever stopped and looked at a primrose? I asked a friend of mine that question recently, and she said, "Yes, there were some on a railway embankment—at least I think they were primroses." She probably passed them at about sixty miles an hour! I don't mean that kind of looking. Nor do I mean the kind of thing the scientist says about a primrose. I am told it is "a dicotyledonous exogen with a five-lobed mono-petalous corolla and central placentation." I prefer Tennyson:

> Flower in the crannied wall,
> I pluck you out of the crannies,
> I hold you here, root and all, in my hand,
> Little flower—but *if* I could understand
> What you are, root and all, and all in all,
> I should know what God and man is.

To look into the face of a primrose and meditate is to understand why Jesus talked as He did about the birds and the lilies. The calm contemplation of God in nature is a rebuke and a remedy in our age of anxiety. "Be not anxious," says Jesus, "consider the lilies of the field."

If we cannot get close to nature, we can contemplate God in His Word. It would be a good thing for some of us to write out a few sentences from the Bible on a card and prop it up near our mirror, so that while we dress in the morning our minds can meditate on the themes they suggest.

"Be still and know that I am God."
"The Lord God omnipotent reigneth."
"The Lord is my Shepherd."
"My peace I give unto you."
"He is able to save to the uttermost."
"The peace of God which passes understanding can stand sentry over our hearts and thoughts."

Christ's message in an age of anxiety surely contains that direction. He Himself had no bogus security of money, no self-esteem that needed the bolstering of another's praise. (Anxiety is so often precipitated by an attack made on our self-esteem.) He looked away to God and is saying to us something like this: "Your Father knows. He understands and cares. He has got your situation in hand. He will tell you what to do. He is the Lord of history, the Master of everything we call accident, the Weaver of all our sins and failures and sorrows into His indestructible plans, and He is the Victor over death."

2. When fighting anxiety consider the value of thankfulness. I am sure it is part of Christ's message. Note how He Himself continually thanked God in what we

must call anxious moments. He said, "Father, I thank Thee that Thou heardest Me." What a profound utterance! He makes an act of thanksgiving about the past at the moment when He desires to banish all doubt and fear about the future from His mind.[1] One could call it a thankful affirmation.

It is a good thing to begin each day thanking God for His many blessings in the past. Could any act be more likely to dispel anxiety feelings than to affirm thankfully what God has done for one in the past? For, clearly, God has not changed, and we thus meet the present and face the future confident that He Who has seen us through in the past will stand by us now.

"His love in time past
Forbids me to think
He'll leave me at last
In trouble to sink;
And each Ebenezer I have in review
Confirms His good pleasure to help me quite through."

Dr. Norman Vincent Peale, of New York, had a letter from a woman whom he was trying to help and whose heart had been full of fear and worry, and of whom he says: "Her life was a pathetic mixture of dissatisfaction, fear, hate and unhappiness." She wrote thus: "My greatest progress dates from the night you told me that 'every day is a good day if you pray.' I began," she says, "to put into practice the idea of affirming that this would be a good day the minute I woke up in the morning, and I can positively say that I haven't had a bad or upsetting day since that time. . . . My days actually haven't been any smoother or any more free from petty annoyances than they ever were, but they just don't seem to have the power to

[1]John 11, 41.

upset me any more. Every night I begin my prayers by
listing all the things for which I am grateful, little things
that happened during the day which added to the happiness
of my day. I know that this habit has geared my mind
to pick out the nice things and forget the unpleasant ones.
The fact that for six weeks I have not had a single bad day
and have refused to get down-hearted with anyone is
really marvellous to me."[1]

The very act of thanking God excludes the devastating
and disintegrating devils of moaning and whining and
grumbling and telling our grievances to all and sundry.
Thankfulness, above all, eliminates the worst devil of all,
self-pity. Let us search our hearts and make sure that
in the premises of our personality there are no meetings
being held of the "Let's be sorry for me" society. That
society has too many branches!

3. Consider thirdly the value of attempting some kind
of service for others. Let us be quite honest with ourselves
and ask ourselves when we did something for another
person which we were not expected to do, or paid for doing,
or from the doing of which we could not expect any personal
prestige for ourselves.

For myself, I have often been shamed out of worry
and anxiety by making myself go to help another—or
try to do so—only to find that that other, so much worse
than I, showed far greater courage with far less reason.

I remember how a woman who had grumbled a dozen
times because her feet ached, was silenced when she visited
another with radiant face and loving heart, who could
move neither hands nor feet, who could not even turn her
head without pain.

Anxious people find that there are hours in which they
simply cannot help thinking about themselves, and this

[1] *The Power of Positive Thinking*, p. 68 (Prentice-Hall Inc., New York).

indeed is not to be laughed at or scorned, for it is nature's way of telling us that there is something wrong within. If the driver of a car hears an unusual rattle, it is generally foolish to drive on. He should stop the car, open the bonnet and seek the cause of the trouble. Introspection, especially with the help of a psychiatrist or minister or doctor, may often guide us to eliminate some trouble which is causing us to look within. But if there is nothing more we can do at any given moment, the way to stop thinking about ourselves is to think of others. If we cannot visit them, we can often write a cheering letter to them, we can always pray for them and that may be the highest form of service one person can do for another.

Further, in many cases of which I have read, sufferers have been healed of their own disabilities when they have sincerely prayed for someone else, though to pray for another with the motive of being healed oneself might well be useless for both. A doctor, who started a prayer circle amongst his patients, writing to *The Church Times*,[1] said, "I noticed that when a woman with headache, giddiness and a dry throat, is asked to pray for a man with cancer, *she at once feels better herself*. She realises that she might have worse diseases, and starts to think about someone else's troubles rather than her own." Job was certainly afflicted with anxiety and he found deliverance through insight (42. 5). How significant is the sentence, "The Lord turned the captivity of Job *when he prayed for his friends*"! (42. 10).

4. Note another step on the way to freedom from anxiety. We must say every day, "Into Thy hands I commit my spirit." What a significant thing St. Luke records of Jesus! "I must go on My way today and tomorrow and the day following."[2] Jesus said that when He was under

---

[1] August 5th, 1955.   Italics mine.
[2] Luke 13, 33.

the threat of murder. Can we every morning make an offering of the day to God, seeking to know and trying to follow His guidance regarding what should be done and said that day? Can we "live a day at a time"? Can we really begin to want *His* way and kill this accursed self-centredness, which even more than any outward factors, like noise or the threat of war, produces anxiety?

There is real freedom in saying to oneself, "This is what God wants me to do today," or even, "This is what He wants me to do during the next hour." If only we can feel that there is a stream of purpose running through our lives and that that stream is as irresistible as the tides, then we can lose our fussy self-importance by yielding ourselves utterly to that purpose, that will, that holy stream. If I am ill, I am still in His hands. If I fail, I am still within His loving purpose. The only real tragedy that can happen to man would be to be spurned by God, but because God is love, that can never happen. Sir Winston Churchill in a solemn speech in Parliament recently said, "When I watch little children playing their merry games, I wonder what will lie before them if God should weary of mankind." But God will never weary of mankind. We have Christ as our assurance on that point. "I will never leave you nor forsake you," is His promise. We may often be frightened, but if we can feel ourselves always within the purposes of God, we shall find peace.

When Anne Sedgwick, the novelist, was seventy years of age, and in such pain and distress that if she sat up her ribs collapsed and she could hardly breathe, and yet when she lay down she could not take the liquid food which she had to sip every half-hour or so, she wrote this: "Life is a queer struggle, but life is beautiful to me. There is joy in knowing that *I lie in the hands of God.*"

This is no easy programme. The pseudo-self is not dethroned so easily. Pride is hard to kill and many are broken before they begin to understand. Men ask for an easy way, and when the way they have to tread is hard, they persuade themselves that they know a short cut. But they never do. Both the world and ourselves were made for God and no way that is not His way is a way through. The only way home is God's way. As Dr. Herbert Gray says: "Our actual world is a difficult and bracing place to live in; and we are all launched into it, whether we will or no, to wrestle and to suffer, and to work till we are weary. It has to be accepted. There is no more futile way of wasting emotion than to groan and complain about its nature. And we are in it because God loves us. Because He would fain see us becoming brave and sturdy spirits, and no less exacting school would produce them. The ultimate end in view is that we should become developed personalities, capable of living in the divine fellowship. And personalities do not develop in soft and easy circumstances."[1]

"Peace, be still," said Jesus on a stormy day at sea, speaking, as I think, not to the waves but to His men, for He knew better than any psychologist how terribly infectious is the emotion of fear, and anyone who cries out in fear and thus spreads that fear amongst the crew of a boat in a heavy storm should be silenced. Actually the Greek word used should be translated, "be muzzled." As we know, the storm abated.

> "The wild winds hushed, the angry deep
> Sank like a little child to sleep."

But later on when His men understood more, they knew that the real secret of inward peace is to forget oneself because one has committed oneself utterly to Him Who

[1] *The Secret of Inward Peace*, p. 13 (Student Christian Movement Press).

cannot be finally defeated. Anxiety disappears when, in the name and power of God, we give ourselves to a purpose and a plan higher and bigger than ourselves.

In later years, when they understood, they would not have been so worried by stormy waves, for at the last they knew that even the bottom of the sea can be the hollow of His hand, and they would have felt safe whatever might have happened to their bodies. By the time martyrdom came to their bodies—as it did—their minds had found the secret of peace.

Slowly, it may be, we too may find the only security there is in the world. When we *know* how precious we are to a God Whose plans can never finally be frustrated, we shall feel safe.

> "Safe when all safety's lost,
>   Safe when men fall,
> And if these poor limbs die,
>   Safest of all."

XI

HELP AT EVERY CORNER

SOME time ago I had the privilege of meeting and speaking with Hugh Redwood. He said that on one occasion, at a time when he was under severe nervous strain, not knowing which way to turn concerning certain decisions he had to make, he was staying at a friend's house previous to speaking at a big meeting. His friend said to him, "You look tired. Would you like to escape all this chatter, and rest in a room upstairs?" Mr. Redwood said that he would like it more than anything else, and to his delight a bright fire was burning, an easy chair was drawn up near it, and at his elbow there was a little table with an open Bible upon it. The Bible was open at Psalm 59, and in the margin opposite verse 10 someone had written in pencil an interpretation which kindled his mind as it does my own. In the Bible we read, "The God of my mercy shall prevent me," where, of course, the word "prevent" means, "go before." But the pencilled interpretation ran thus: "My God in His lovingkindness *shall meet me at every corner*." Mr. Redwood said that it came to him as light in a dark place, light from the very heart of God. It cheered him immensely. He made his decision. He turned his corner successfully. Mr. Redwood is ageing now and has just retired from a long and useful career as a journalist in Fleet Street, but young or old, the message is for us all.

Side by side with that story, I should like to put one about my own early life. In 1915 I left Richmond College at the age of twenty-one to take charge of a small church in Surrey. It seems ridiculous now for a boy of twenty-one to take charge of a church and preach Sunday by Sunday to people who know so much more about life, and most of them a great deal more about God than he could possibly know. The thing that terrified me most was the prospect of having to take a funeral, and the worst came to the worst, for my first funeral was the funeral of a little child. There is something seemly in the death of the very aged, but the death of a child is so shattering that I thought the parents must resent the intrusion of a healthy young boy like myself into the intimate places of their grief. I confided my dismay to my Superintendent Minister, half hoping that he would offer to take it for me. But he knew better and I think I shall never forget what he said. "You will find," he said, "that God is there to meet you. He is in those circumstances now before you get there, and He will not let you down." On the strength of that message I got past that difficult corner.

So there is the testimony of an old man and the testimony of a young man. "My God in His lovingkindness will meet me at every corner."

In this chapter I propose to consider some of those corners which we all have to turn, corners which cause us anxiety, and try to show how our religion can help us to meet them.

There are certain psychologists who remind us that life is full of what they call "menaces." They use the word in a technical sense, but by it they mean that all the way through life there is something just round the corner which will make a demand of a special kind on us when we meet it. We have not got to it yet, perhaps, but we know that it is imminent. The mastery of the art of living depends on whether we can turn our corner with serenity and courage, or whether we turn it in anxiety and dread.

These menaces begin even in our childhood. Let us imagine a home in which there are little children. The first goes to school. Then the second goes to school. The third is made aware of what is perhaps his first menace; at least his first since that very real one of having to be born into this wicked world at all! He knows that soon he will not be able to decide whether to play in the garden or whether to play indoors. *He must go to school.* I cannot tell you how important it is, for the whole of his later life, to help him turn that first corner with courage and serenity. If, through teasing or misrepresentation, he dreads it, his parents may fasten on him a "pattern of reaction" which can determine his attitude to the unknown for the rest of his life. I have tried psychologically to help grown-up people whose fear-reaction to anything that is strange and unknown was determined because they were made to dread going to school.

It is not too early in the life of a child about to go to school, to speak of the Friend Who will stand by him at every corner. If you care to read a novel by Hugh Walpole called *The Golden Scarecrow*, you will find in it how wonderfully a little child can derive comfort and strength from that unseen Friend, Who is indeed a Friend for little children, not "above the bright blue sky," but comfortingly and reassuringly near.

As childhood moves on, another decision has to be made. Round the corner is that decision, rather dreaded by many children, of what they are going to be. If parents with children of that age are reading these words, I do implore them to allow their child, within reason, to do what he wants to do. In any case, do not decide in ten minutes the life-work of another human being for the next fifty years. The happy people are those who like doing what

their daily work compels them to do. It is sad to think
that so many of our fellows watch the clock all day, and
only begin to live when it says half past five or six. Yet
so many parents are blind to this and say, "Oh, he can go
into my office! Oh, she can learn typing and shorthand!"
when the child is very eager for something else, to be a
nurse, for instance, and too shy or frightened to say so.
Many children are far too shy and too afraid of their parents'
disapproval to do anything but concur in what their parents
think they ought to do. There is an understandable idea
about that a family name in a business should be perpetuated.
It is an idea that can be very selfish. After all, is there any
real reason why Tompkins and Company should go on
for ever with a new Tompkins at the head of it in each
generation? It is much more important that a human being
should be happy. Let us give these young people freedom
and tell them that God is their Friend, that He really is a
Guide, that He will meet them at every corner and will
not allow them to go down the wrong street. That is a
far better fulfilment of our parental obligation than forcing
upon them a career which will become a prison.

Let us think now of the young girl, and indeed of the
young man, contemplating marriage. That is a very
difficult corner for a great many young people. They
are not sure whether they are in love. They are not sure
whether they will meet someone else whom they will like
better. A girl is frequently inwardly distressed concerning all the demands that will be made upon her. Our
dreams, as you know, still reveal our inner disquietude.
Here is a dream recounted in Dr. Maurice Nicoll's book,
Dream Psychology. A girl of seventeen continually dreamed
that a soldier called at the door of her parents' home, and
when she answered it, grabbed her by the arm, took her
down "our street," and then round a corner into a street
she did not know. It was so strange and perplexing and

the traffic was so confusing that she said, "I always wake up crying."

Here, clearly, is a young girl afraid of the next corner. Subconsciously she knows that she will have to leave the familiar home-life where everything is familiar, and in the company of a comparatively strange man turn a corner into an unknown, confusing street. Here is the chance for a real mother—if the dream is related to her—to come in with advice and help about that difficult matter called sex-experience which so many youngsters both dread and desire. We saw earlier that dread and desire are so frequently the factors which produce anxiety (p. 33). Here is the occasion for one of those intimate chats between mothers and daughters, and fathers and sons. What a chance to tell her about the Friend Who will meet her at every corner, and to lift sex high above the murky atmosphere of the furtive secret or the obscene joke into the same sunshine as flowers and health and beauty and holiness!

A word must be said to those who do not marry. Frankly, I think it is a disgrace that in so many circles fun is made of the unmarried woman between forty and sixty. Again and again, she is the subject of feeble jokes which are much more cruel than they are funny. My experience is that wherever unselfish and fine work is being done in this land of ours, you will find women of that age doing it. I do not know what my own church would do without these women. Many of them must feel frustrated and disappointed, and the problem is largely due to the fact that so many men of their generation have been killed. They are trying to work off their creative energies in work for other people, and they are trying to express an imprisoned love in the service of the world. All honour to them! They will turn the corner of unmarried middle age successfully if they accept themselves and take God into partnership. Let us not forget that the first law of mental health and ınward peace is to be honest with oneself. How wonderfully God can come into that situation, for He is the God of truth and utter sincerity! "My God in His loving-kindness shall meet me at every corner."

Then, as we grow to be old, let us not be amongst those who cling with clutching hands to the wheel long after we can drive the car successfully. How often we men cling to the directorship of a business when there are young men just behind us who could do it so much better! How many times have the elderly failed to turn the corner and driven a business into the ditch! Blessed is he who knows when to retire and who has the strength of mind to do so. We who are ageing can turn this corner successfully, and even very old people, with the wisdom they have gathered through the years and the mellow temper which life ought by now to have attained, can be assets in any situation. But let us not shrink from the corner, but take it in courage and serenity. Our God will meet us at every corner.

It is strange that before the word "menace" was adopted by psychologists, W. E. Henley, the poet, should use it in their sense:

> Beyond this place of wrath and tears
>   Looms but the horror of the shade,
> And yet the menace of the years
>   Finds and shall find me unafraid.

If we are to meet "the menace of the years" without anxiety, I think we must make a kind of pact with death. That should not be a morbid thing to write. It is certainly no good pretending that we shall never die, and as the years pass we must not allow ourselves to adopt the same attitude as the child who dreads school. After all, why should we be afraid? Death is as natural an incident as birth. If we had had the consciousness, we should have dreaded being born. It would have been terrifying to give up that secure and comfortable pre-natal world for this cold, harsh world into which we came at birth. But there were arms to receive us, eyes that smiled at us, and all the comfort we needed. Will He Who saw us round the first corner, desert us at the last one? Does He not understand that we are easily frightened, and will He not come to our aid?

Let me tell you, as one who has witnessed many deaths, that in my experience I have never seen one that was unhappy. Sometimes there is fear *beforehand*, and pain, too, but the end is either sudden and over before we can register any emotion, or else we enter the complete pain-lessness of sleep, *or else it is one of the most joyous experiences we can undergo.* I sat once on the bed of a man who was dying and his hand lay within my own. I must have gripped his hand more tightly than I thought, for he said a strange thing to me. "Don't pull me back," he said, "it looks so wonderful further on." And when my own sister was thought to be dying, she overheard the doctor say to the nurse, "She won't get through the night." The patient heard it as the best news in the world. When later the nurse said, "She is going to pull through after all," my sister told us afterwards that she heard the words with regret.

Lazarus, they say, was a melancholy man to the end of his days, and if there were space I could bring you an immense amount of evidence to support the dictum of William Hunter, the famous doctor, who on his death-bed said, "If I had strength enough to hold a pen, I would write how easy and pleasant a thing it is to die."[1] "My God in His lovingkindness shall meet us at every corner." Surely we may add, especially the last!

[1] I have printed some of this evidence in *Why Do Men Suffer* : (Student Christian Movement Press), Chapter 12, "Is Death a Calamity?" pp.234ff.

I want to condition my mind in such a way that when my last heart-beats tap at the door of eternity, I shall feel as I feel when the taxi-cab man knocks on the door of my home to take me off for a holiday.

I love my work and it is good for a person like me to have to do certain things by a certain time. But how I love my holidays; the feeling that the hall can fill with letters and I shan't have to read them—not yet anyway; that the phone can ring all day, but I shan't have to answer it!

So let us mentally and spiritually prepare for the journey and pack *only those things we shall need*, and be ready to enjoy a fuller life. For let us remember that those whom we foolishly call the dead are far more alive than we are. They are beyond the fog and dirt and clouds of the smoky earth-cities. They are out on the great mountains of experience, with the infinite sky above them and the never-fading sunshine round about them; there, where the great winds blow, and men breathe an air we have never known and look upon a loveliness which we have never seen. "Eye hath not seen, nor ear heard, neither hath it entered into the heart of man to conceive those things which God hath prepared for them that love Him."

Do you know the lines which the poet, John Oxenham, put into the mouth of a man who was afraid to die? Listen!

> Shapeless and grim
> A shadow dim
> O'erhung my ways
> And darkened all my days,
> And those who saw,
> With bated breath,
> Said, "Hush! this is death."

And I in weakness,
Slipping toward the night,
In sore affright
Looked up, and lo, no spectre grim,
But just a dim
Sweet face.   A sweet, high, mother face,
A face like Christ's own mother's face,
Alight with tenderness and grace.

"Thou art not Death," I cried,
For life's supremest fantasy
Had never thus envisaged Death to me:
"Thou art not Death—the End."
In accents winning came the answer, "Friend,
There is no Death.
I am the Beginning, not the End."

It is a strange thing that the idea ever arose concerning
the Christian religion, that adherence to it would be a
kind of insurance policy against suffering. The things
that happen to other people will happen to us, and people
who demand immunity from trouble are asking that God
should have planned life on a different, and I must add, an
inferior, basis.

When I was a schoolboy I hated school, and my troubles
were not lessened by the fact that I sat next to a boy whom
I then regarded as the luckiest boy on earth. He had such
a kind, indulgent father. If the weather were sunny,
my schoolmate was allowed to play in the fields, and when
the examinations came, which I dreaded from my youth
up, he was allowed to stay away. All that happened *then*
was that the master wrote on his report in red ink, "Absent
from Examination." That didn't seem very serious! My
cruel, heartless father demanded that I should go to school
however lovely the weather, and that I should turn up at

examinations, however hard they were! But now I am grateful. I know now who had the better father. So often we say to God, "Why don't You let me off? I only want to be happy." But those of us who have thought God cruel and heartless, will one day say, "I am glad I learnt what I did learn in the school of life." And as my dear father, whom now I revere, did not let me escape school, but stood by me through its childish troubles, so my heavenly Father is too good to let me off, too trustworthy to let me down, and too loving to let me go.

If we had paid attention to the words of Jesus, we should never have got this silly idea that religion would let us off. Listen to this: "Men will hand you over to suffer affliction, and they will kill you, and you will be hated by all outsiders for My sake."[1] "You will be flogged in the synagogues and brought before governors and kings for My sake."[2] "The hour cometh that whosoever killeth you shall think that he offereth service unto God."[3]

I think I ought to remind the reader that the end of St. Mark's Gospel which talks about people treading on snakes and not being bitten, and drinking deadly things without taking harm, is not an authentic part of the gospel. St. Mark's Gospel was passed round the young churches in a long roll of papyrus, and we can imagine how tremendously popular it must have been. The result was that the end of it got worn out and torn and finally lost. The authentic gospel of Mark finishes at Chapter XVI, verse 9. The rest has been added by another hand. But here is an authentic note of truth: "I heard a great Voice out of the throne saying, Behold the tabernacle of God is with men, and He shall dwell *with them* and they shall be His people, and God Himself shall be *with them* and be their

[1] Matthew 24, 9.
[2] Mark 13, 9.
[3] John 16, 2.

God."[1] That Presence means something greater than immunity. *It means the transmuting of our troubles into our training, and the changing of our liabilities into assets.*

During the First World War a soldier in the trenches saw his friend out in no-man's-land (the ground between our trenches and those of the enemy) stumble and fall in the hail of bullets. He said to his officer, "May I go, sir, and bring him in?" But the officer refused. "No one can live out there," he said. "I should only lose you as well." Disobeying the order, the man went to try to save his friend, for they had been like David and Jonathan throughout the whole war. Somehow he got his friend on to his shoulder and staggered back to the trenches, but he himself lay mortally wounded and his friend was dead. The officer was angry. "I told you not to go," he said. "Now I have lost both of you. It was not worth it." With his dying breath the man said, "But it was worth it, sir." "Worth it!" said the officer. "How could it be? Your friend is dead and you are mortally wounded." The boy shrank from the reproach, but looking up into his officer's face, he said, "It was worth it, sir, because when I got to him, he said, 'Jim, I knew you'd come.'"

Yes, God does not say, "I will excuse you from passing through the waters." He says, "When you pass through the waters, I shall be there too." "My God in His loving-kindness shall meet you at every corner." Yes, every corner of anxiety or temptation, or sorrow, or pain, or loss, until the last corner of all, for "though I walk through the valley of the shadow of death, I will fear no evil for *Thou art with me.*"

[1] Revelation 21, 3.

XII

HELP FROM THE OTHER SIDE

THE last chapter aimed at giving help to those who from time to time, when they have to take a difficult "corner," feel a sense of anxiety and personal insecurity. But there are many who feel a sense of *cosmic* insecurity. They ask continually an ancient and famous question, "Is the universe friendly?" My own answer is not only an emphatic affirmative but I would maintain that the nature of the invisible world apprehended by faith and by mystical experience is man's final defence against anxiety.

The aim of this chapter is to help us recover our sense of the reality and ultimate friendliness of the spiritual world; the world that is all around us, the world from which we have come and to which we must return, the world to which we really belong. These material bodies and brains are instruments which we have to use as means of manifestation in this particular phase of being. Without disparaging them, I am sure that many of us have heard voices from the shore of that other, much more real world. When we hear them we know that we are "strangers and pilgrims here below,"[1] and that we are "a colony of heaven,"[2] that we belong to a world of friendliness, peace and joy.

> "And when the strife is fierce, the warfare long,
> Steals on the ear the distant triumph-song,
> And hearts are brave again, and arms are strong."

[1] Hebrews 11, 13.
[2] Philippians 3, 20.

Let us pause for a moment while we ask ourselves what we mean by the word "real." I call the spiritual world the real world because although the material world, in which we live, has a reality of a kind, it is only temporary. A thing like love, for example, or a thing like truth, has a more permanent reality than any material object. Jesus recognised this when He said, "The heavens and the earth shall pass away, but My word shall not pass away."[1] F. H. Bradley, the learned and famous author of *Appearance and Reality*, said, "The man who demands a reality more solid than that of the religious consciousness, knows not what he seeks." A great many people use the word "real" to mean the things that they can touch, see, hear, taste, and smell; things, in a word, the apparent reality of which reaches them through their senses. But we must not suppose that the universe ends at the point at which our senses cease to register it. The things we touch and taste and smell and hear and see are only shadows compared with the reality of the things that lie just beyond the grasp of the senses.

Plato, at the beginning of Book 7 of the *Republic*, has a much-quoted, but very interesting, parable in which he teaches that man's knowledge of the world is that of an observer chained from childhood and facing inwards into a cave and unable to turn his head. Shadows move across the roof of the cave from real objects behind him, but, imprisoned as he is, he cannot see them. He can only see the shadows.[2] The world that is truly real we do not *see* at all. We only see the shadows that are thrown by it. Wordsworth followed Plato in supposing that every beautiful thing is a kind of shadow of a yet more beautiful reality in the unseen world, and it is to that unseen world that we

[1] Mark 13, 31.

[2] *Republic of Plato*, A. D. Lindsay's translation, pp. 235 ff. (J. M. Dent).

truly belong. When beautiful music makes us cry, or when the account of some heroic deed touches our heart, our feelings are really those of nostalgia or homesickness. We have come from a world to which we still belong, where the reality that is behind music and behind unselfish love is the dominating factor. Seeing the shadows we long for the substance. Hearing the echo—which we call great music—we long for the reality which perhaps once we knew, and certainly shall know later.

Probably we should agree that what we take to be the nature of reality depends on the state of the mind at any given moment. For example, a baby lives in our world and has all five senses, but in early days little is real to him save milk, physical comfort and warmth and vaguely the person who gives them to him. A dog lives in the same world as ourselves and he has all the five senses which we possess, but he does not enter into life to the extent that we do. I am told that what he sees is less colourful than the world we see, that what he hears is less important than what he smells. When we consider the birds, we may recall that they hear sounds which we cannot hear, and in one sense live in what is a smaller world, and, in another sense, a bigger world than ourselves. I am told that a bat finds its way by emitting a note so high that the human ear cannot pick it up, but as the bat flies and throws out this humanly inaudible sound, the reverberation of that sound from solid objects enables him to fly safely without dashing himself against hard substances which he cannot readily see. If you bandage the eyes of a bat, he can still find his way, but if you stop up his ears, he cannot. In other words, he lives in our world and yet it is quite different because of the state of his receptive apparatus. Similarly, of course, the beetle must live in quite a different world from ourselves. It is odd to think of things which may live in our homes, and yet do not know anything about us who give them hospitality! We could extend the idea to fantastic limits. A spider on a church pillar probably finds it a problem of immense importance to negotiate, shall we say, a small crack in the plaster. What does he know of the church? How can he know anything of what a church is for, or of the street beyond, let alone the city beyond that, or the country, or the world. . . .

Is it not most likely that we are living a little insect life, shut in by the limitations of our nature from understanding what the universe is about? We are like savages who see marks in a book, can count them and classify those that look the same, *but who cannot read the book*. We think we are clever to discover the stars, to multiply speed, to discover radar, and release atomic energy, but can we know anything of the meaning and extent of the spiritual universe that lies behind anything which the senses can ever discover?

Probably if we could be given one extra sense, we should know at once that the world is full of spiritual presences. We sing about

> "Angel voices ever singing
> Round Thy throne of light,"

but it is only a guess, in the dark. We live in the comparatively grey world of the senses, and for the most part are shut up by the five prison bars which enclose us all.

I want to suggest that probably the life we live here is very much the nature of a dream. When you are dreaming, your dream *seems* real. When you are dreaming, you never think, "I am only dreaming." When you wake up you say, "I *was* dreaming." As long as the dream lasts, the people you meet in your dream are as real as yourself. We should begin to make some progress in apprehending the reality of the spiritual world if we realised that death is probably like waking up. We only call this life real because we cannot at will get out of it into any other. But the point of awakening, even if we have been dreaming all night, makes the dream transient and almost momentary and certainly unreal compared with the waking life. How many times, on waking, have we said, "It was only a dream"? That is probably what we shall say about this life when we awaken at the point that is stupidly called death. When we wake up in the real world, this life, even if we have lived to be a hundred, will seem momentary, transient and unreal.

How wonderfully the poets say these things for us! Listen to Shelley writing about his dear, dead friend, Keats:

> Peace, peace! He is not dead, he doth not sleep—
> He hath awakened from the dream of life. . . .
> He has outsoared the shadow of our night;
> Envy and calumny and hate and pain,
> And that unrest which men miscall delight,
> Can touch him not and torture not again;
> From the contagion of the world's slow stain
> He is secure . . .
> He lives, he wakes—'tis death is dead, not he.

Or listen to this!

> Out of the sleep of Earth
>   With visions rife,
> I woke in Death's clear morning
>   Full of Life,
> And said to God,
> Whose smile made all things bright,
> "That was an awful dream I had last night."

If you have had a happy life, you will wake up at death and say, "I have had such a lovely dream." If you have had a sad life, you will wake up and say, perhaps, "That was an awful dream I had last night." But it will have gone just like a dream. It only seemed real when we were dreaming. As Charles Wesley said, "Our life is a dream." We should be wise never to imagine that it is real with the reality which eternity will reveal.

Now when we say that life is a dream, we do not, of course, mean that it is unimportant. Dreams are very important. I am convinced myself that they will take in the near future the importance they used to have in Bible days. All through that Holy Book you read of God speaking to men in dreams. It was through a dream that the Baby Jesus escaped the violence of Herod. It was through another dream that Jesus was brought back from Egypt (Matthew 2. 13, 19). And God has not changed. He has not "given all that up now"! He still tries to get His messages through our dreams.

At the beginning of the century, Freud published his great book on the interpretation of dreams and he has made a unique contribution to man's assessment of a dream's importance. The passing dream may be of passing moment, but certainly the repeated dream is a voice to be heeded I must testify that again and again a vivid dream, written down immediately, has given me insight into factors within my own life which have influenced important decisions. Similarly, the dream which we call the earth life is important, but not less a dream.

Of course, when people ask us for evidences of the existence of that other shore, it is usually impossible to give them evidence which is not subjective, that is to say, limited to the experience of the person concerned. But, then, that is true in other situations which do not call for doubt, or involve the shrugged shoulder or the lifted eyebrow. For example, many of our men, during the two wars, went to the medical officer and said, "I have a pain." No one could prove it or disprove it. If a man says, "I feel remorse," there may be other symptoms which point to the truth of what he is saying, but no one can prove it or disprove it. Yet we do not usually doubt that these experiences happen. When a man says he is in love, no scientific test can be applied to prove or to disprove his statement. So it is with the evidence of what we call mystical experience, by which I mean insight into reality not adducible by the senses or by any process of reason.

Consider how much of the Bible we should have to tear up if, for lack of scientific evidence, we denied the reality of mystical experiences. Elisha was full of fears until he perceived the horses and chariots of another world. The young man with him could see nothing until, in answer to the prophet's prayer, his eyes were opened. "And behold the mountain was full of horses and chariots of fire round about Elisha."[1] Who was the fourth man in the flames which left no mark on those three mighty men whose story is told in the book of Daniel? Which of the five senses was Nebuchadnezzar using when he rose up in haste and said to his counsellors, "Did we not cast three men bound into the midst of the fire?" They answered and said unto the king, "True, O king." He answered and said, "Lo, I see four men loose, walking in the midst of the fire and they have no hurt; and the shape of the fourth is like the Son of God."[2]

Was Jesus romancing when He spake of the twelve legions of angels who so easily could have come to His rescue and left His enemies gibbering in terror?[3] Is it

[1] II Kings 6, 17.

[2] Daniel 3, 24-5.

[3] Matthew 26, 53.

poetry without any reference to fact that speaks of an angel who ministered to Him in the desert and comforted Him in the Garden?[1] And are we ourselves talking nonsense when, at what seems to me the climax of the Communion Service, we say together, "Therefore with angels and archangels and all the company of heaven, we laud and magnify Thy glorious name, evermore praising Thee, and saying, Holy, Holy, Holy"?

Spiritualism will help us in this matter of voices from the further shore, when, with greater confidence, it learns how to separate the chaff from the grain; when its experiments can exclude the fraudulent trickster and the unconsciously duped medium. But without any recourse to Spiritualism, there are probably many people who, having lost their dear ones and seeking no help from mediums, know, beyond a shadow of doubt that their so-called dead are more alive than ever they were, and who have a communion with them too rich for communication.

We can always deny a mystic experience by saying, "I have never heard any voice from that other shore," but we can never turn on another and say, "Neither have you," and locked up in many a heart, too sensitive and shy to speak of it, is the secret conviction that very near to us, especially at some moments and in some moods, is a world more real than any reality we know through the senses.

When I talk about the mystics, I do not mean only those we read of in the lives of the saints. Many people have experiences of mysticism who have not been prepared for those experiences by religious meditation or prayer. Indeed, many people have had mystical experiences thrust

[1] Matthew 4, 11; Luke 22, 43.

upon them when they themselves have been almost indifferent to religion. Frankly, this gives me a sense of comfort and reassurance. It sounds as though by whatever road we may have come, and however far we may have strayed from the invisible country to which we truly belong, we retain the power to apprehend its reality given certain conditions, conditions which are not necessarily linked with religion.

No one, I presume, would have called Winifred Holtby a deeply religious person or a mystic. She was a happy, able, young woman, with a glorious gift of writing English, and she died at the age of thirty-seven. When she was thirty-two the doctors told her that she had only a few more years to live. Her spirit rose up in rebellion against the bodily illness that made it impossible for her to carry out her ambition. One day, feeling unhappy and depressed, she was walking up a hill in Buckinghamshire and came to a trough of water outside a farmyard. The surface was frozen over and with her stick she broke the ice to allow some lambs to have a drink. Listen to Vera Brittain telling us the story! "She broke the ice for them with her stick, and as she did so, she heard a voice within her say, 'Having nothing, yet possessing all things.' It was so distinct that she looked round startled, but she was alone with the lambs on the top of the hill. Suddenly, in a flash, the grief, the bitterness, the sense of frustration disappeared; all desire to possess power and glory for herself vanished away and never came back. . . . The moment of conversion—as she called it with tears in her eyes—was the supreme spiritual experience of her life. She always associated it afterwards with the words of Bernard Bosanquet on salvation: 'And now we are saved absolutely, we need not say from what, *we are at home in the universe*, and, in principle and in the main, feeble and timid creatures as we are, there is nothing anywhere within the world or without it that can make us afraid.'"[1]

How true are the lines of Sidney Royse Lysaght!

> We have dreamed dreams beyond our comprehending,
> Visions too beautiful to be untrue;
> We have seen mysteries that yield no clue,
> And sought our goals on ways that have no ending. . . .
> We have seen loveliness that shall not pass;
> We have beheld immortal destinies. . . .
> Ay, we whose flesh shall perish as the grass
> Have flung the passion of the heart that dies
> Into the hope of everlasting life.[2]

And it is not just a life that is everlasting in the sense merely of duration. It is life in a different dimension with a different atmosphere about it; from which all anxiety and fear are banished. For this life the soul longs and in longing sometimes gets a foretaste. It is this foretaste to which C. S. Lewis in his autobiography[3] gives the name "joy." Suddenly, and apparently without warning, as he "stood beside a flowering currant bush on a summer day," there came over him a sense of "Milton's 'enormous bliss.'" He writes: "Before I knew what I desired, the desire itself was gone, the whole glimpse withdrawn, the world turned commonplace again, or only stirred by a longing for the longing that had just ceased. It had taken only a moment of time; and in a certain sense everything else that had ever happened to me was insignificant in comparison."[4] Of a similar experience he wrote: "In this experience also there was the same surprise and the same

---

[1] *The Testament of Friendship*, p. 325 (Macmillan). (Italics mine.)

[2] *Horizons and Landmarks.*

[3] C. S. Lewis, *Surprised by Joy* (Geoffrey Bles, 1955).

[4] *Op. cit.* p. 22.

sense of incalculable importance. It was something quite different from ordinary life and even from ordinary pleasure; something, as they would now say, 'in another dimension.'"[1] He describes the experience as "*an unsatisfied desire which is itself more desirable than any other satisfaction*," and says that it has one outstanding characteristic, "that anyone who has experienced it will want it again." Yet no one can engineer the experience. "Joy," he says, "is never a possession, always a desire for something longer ago, or further away, or still 'about to be.'"[2]

I have myself known a few such experiences. One seems taken out of the ordinary world, or rather, the ordinary world is illumined by a supernatural radiance. One feels an indescribable sense of well-being and deep joy. One is at home in a friendly universe, and though the experience may only last a moment, and one longs again and again that it might happen again, not only does one never forget that it did happen, but life is never the same again. One is sure that one is safe, that all is well, that God is good, that the final significance of the universe is friendly to all that we value most, that the sacred values like love, truth, humility, and unselfishness will triumph over all evil whatever appearances may suggest to the contrary and however blatant and powerful may seem the temporary sway of pride and greed and selfishness, and that all things work together towards an indescribable good to all men who do not finally say "No" to God.

My friend, Dr. Raynor Johnson, in his book, *The Imprisoned Splendour*, has collected a whole series of mystical experiences, and they—and indeed the whole book—are well worth study.[3] John Buchan, for example, tells an experience of which he says, "One seemed to be a happy

[1] *Op. cit.* p. 23.
[2] *Op. cit.* p. 79.
[3] See especially pp. 300 ff. (Hodder & Stoughton).

part of a friendly universe." He speaks of having, again and again, what he calls "the hour of revelation" and "a glimpse of the peace of eternity."[1] Note also the phrase, "the hour of knowing", in Rupert Brooke's poem "The Vision"[2]

> And I knew
> That this was the hour of knowing,
> And the night and the woods and you
> Were one together, and I should find
> Soon in the silence the hidden key
> Of all that had hurt and puzzled me—
> Why you were you, and the night was kind.
> And the woods were part of the heart of me.
> And there I waited breathlessly,
> Alone; and slowly the holy three,
> The three that I loved, together grew
> One, in the hour of knowing,
> Night, and the woods, and you—

Hugh Walpole, meditating on the certainty of death and the lovely things he would have to leave, says, "Then with absolute conviction I was aware that I would be leaving nothing, that whatever I had found lovely and of good report I should still enjoy."[3] A friend of Raynor Johnson, writing down his experiences during a bombing raid by the Japanese, wrote, "I didn't want to be killed. . . . But I knew that if I were killed, it would be absolutely all right, not because there would be nothingness, but because there would be goodness and richer experience beyond the grave. . . . I felt as though some unseen power were about me, wholly friendly, and I knew without the shadow of doubt, that at the back of this strife was sheer goodness, and that though this did not imply

---

[1] *Memory Hold the Door*, pp. 120–1.

[2] Rupert Brooke, *The Complete Poems* (Sidgwick & Jackson).

[3] Hugh Walpole, *My Religious Experience* (Ernest Benn).

immunity from danger or death, these things somehow were insignificant and irrelevant. . . . It didn't seem to matter what happened—it was all right beyond."[1] C. F. Andrews says of an experience, "A veil seemed to be lifted from my eyes. I found the world wrapped in an inexpressible glory with its waves of joy and beauty bursting and breaking on all sides. . . . There was nothing and no one whom I did not love at that moment." Another writes, "I felt happiness and peace beyond words." William de Morgan, on listening to a symphony of Beethoven, says, "If reality is like that *I have no cause to be anxious or afraid*." And, of course, we could go on quoting similar experiences too numerous and too sincere to be dismissed. All the writers who have these mystical experiences speak of a sense of exultation, of "immense joyousness," of "a living presence." "I knew," says Dr. R. M. Bucke, "that the universe is so built and ordered that without any peradventure all things work together for the good of each and all, that the foundation principle of the world is what we call love, and that the happiness of every individual is in the long run absolutely certain."[2]

Raynor Johnson says of these experiences that "all those who even for a moment have glimpsed this ineffable world have longed all their waking days to recapture the experience." And we find that all these experiences have certain things in common. We must not dwell on them, but it is worth listing them.

1. There is a sense of what cannot be called anything else but unity with God.

2. There is a sense that the universe is, in spite of much evidence to the contrary, finally friendly.

3. There is a sense that one loves all men and that a fellowship is in course of being created in which all souls

[1] Raynor Johnson, *Op. cit.* p. 31 (Hodder & Stoughton).

[2] *Cosmic Consciousness*, pp. 73–4 (Dutton & Co.).

will dwell together in mutual love and happiness, anxiety and fear having been done away.

4. There is a sense that the true values in life will be vindicated and established.

5. Above all, there is a sense of absolute conviction which I cannot express differently than by saying that all is well, and that at last all of us will feel and know that all is well.   Having written that down, I came across a saying of Lady Julian of Norwich, "All will be well, and all will be well, and all manner of things will be well."

When I say, "All is well," I mean that the way God runs His world, a way which so often puzzles and bewilders us, giving rise to doubt or fear or even resentment, will not only be approved by us, but be seen to be so utterly right as to call out feelings of adoration and praise for which language is utterly inadequate.   If reality is like that, there is certainly no rational basis for anxiety.

For some this chapter will seem to be remote from life.   In a sense it *is* remote from the hurly-burly of bus-catching, typewriter-tapping, selling goods over the counter, making money, and so on.   But I hope that for some it may seem more relevant to life than many a message that sets out to deal with our everyday doings.   If we could realise the reality of the unseen world, if we could hear the voices from the other shore, we should know that we are in the hands of a Power, utterly loving, utterly understanding, utterly wise, utterly forgiving, finally omnipotent.   We should know that we are what St. Paul called "accepted in the beloved," and even now we should glimpse a joy so deep and transforming that there are no words for it.   We should exult in it and feel exalted by it.

Shakespeare spoke of death as "That undiscovered country from whose bourne no traveller returns."   Well, I am glad it is not fully discovered and mapped out or there would be nothing fresh about the future, but I should like to think that what has been written earlier has helped to take away from some hearts the fear of death, either our own or that of our loved ones.   For it really will be wonderful to wake up and find the sunshine coming through the windows of the house of new beginnings that lies at the end of the dusty road we call life on earth.   And who said it was an undiscovered country?   One Traveller came back, and it is reported that when He did so, He said, "All hail!"   In Greek it is one word which is not only a greeting but a report, and the word means "Rejoice!"   Surely that was an authentic Voice from the other shore, and all the lesser voices say the same thing. They speak of peace and love and never-ending joy.   So let us not be afraid any more.   This life is only a dream.   One day we shall wake up, and say, with one of old, words filled with a new, radiant and transcendent significance, "When I awake, I am still with Thee."

> So, let us turn to the unfinished task
> That earth demands, strive for one hour to keep
> A watch with God, nor watching fall asleep,
> Before immortal destinies we ask.
> Before we seek to share
> A larger purpose, a sublimer care,
> *Let us o'ercome the bondage of our fears,*
> And fit ourselves to bear
> The burden of our few and sinful years.
> Ere we would claim a right to comprehend
> The meaning of the life that has no end
> Let us be faithful to our passing hours,
> And read their beauty, and that light pursue
> Which gives the dawn its rose, the noon its blue,
> And tells its secret to the wayside flowers.

[1] Sidney Royse Lysaght, "*Horizons and Landmarks,*" p.123 (Macmillan.)
Italics mine.

APPENDICES

APPENDIX I

EVERYMAN'S HOUSE OF PRAYER
(*A Way of Prayer, for Busy People*)

I HAVE added this appendix because this way of praying has been of help to me. Others, however, who have got settled and satisfying ways of praying, will not need it and can pass it by. I have a secret hope that some may find it the most useful chapter in the book. St. Paul says that prayer is the way to deal with anxiety. When he himself was in prison, he wrote to the Christians at Philippi: "In nothing be anxious, but in everything by prayer and supplication with thanksgiving let your requests be made known unto God." Paul promises that if we do this, the peace of God, which passes all understanding, will stand sentry over our hearts and thoughts.[1] And that is just what the anxious person needs, a guarded mind, kept quiet and serene in the innermost cell of being, whatever turmoil may be going on around him.

Every serious Christian recognises that prayer is essential. We are compelled to admit that it comes easier to some than to others. Perhaps reluctantly we are compelled to admit that to *pray* well demands as much practice and self-discipline as to *play* well on an instrument and that we have not done much about it. Probably all Christian people pray a little and have some kind of traffic with heaven, even if it is only a faint kind of thanksgiving for the beauties of nature or the love of a friend. Surely if *all* commerce with heaven ended, the soul would die. Science, at any rate, knows nothing of an organism permanently cut off from its

[1] Philippians 4, 6–7.

environment and remaining alive. Jesus Himself felt the need of prayer, taught prayer and practised prayer. We cannot leave praying to the experts and say, "Well, prayer isn't much in my line."

Yet there is not much reality about prayer for many of us. We "say our prayers," but for some it is a matter of the Lord's Prayer and a few petitions, taken perhaps unchanged from childhood's days. Let us honestly ask ourselves what we should do with half an hour if we decided to spend it in prayer? If we can satisfyingly answer the question, nothing more needs to be said. But many have no method, and the ways of others leave them unhelped. They would echo a little known verse of Cowper:

> The saints are comforted, I know,
>   And love Thy house of prayer;
> I therefore go where others go,
>   But find no comfort there.

They would like to pray, but they do not know how to go about it. The Roman Catholic has his daily Prime and Compline. The Anglican has his Prayer Book. The Quaker is trained to use a silence and we can gather help from them all, and yet perhaps the reader does not feel at home in any of these disciplines.

I myself felt in great need of a method, and I have devised one which has been of use to me, and I would like to pass it on in case others may find it useful. It owes a lot to some words of Dr. Fosdick in his book, *Successful Christian Living*.[1] It owes a lot to a conversation I had with my friend the Rev. John Carter during a northern preaching tour.

Let us think for a moment of our Lord's advice to the men and women of His day: "Enter into your inner room." I have often pondered over that word, because very few, if any, of His hearers would have an inner room. There is

[1] Student Christian Movement Press, 1937. See page 19.

evidence that Jesus Himself lived in a one-roomed house. Did He not speak, for example, of putting the lamp on the lampstand that it might give light to "all that are in the house"?[1] That surely implied a one-roomed house. I am sure Jesus would never use language which only applied to rich folk. Then it dawned on my literal, Western mind that He meant *an imaginative room*.

I cannot trace who wrote these lines, but they express just what I mean.

> There is a viewless, cloistered room,
>   As high as heaven, as fair as day,
> Where, though my feet may join the throng,
>   My soul can enter in, and pray.
>
> One hearkening, even, cannot know
>   When I have crossed the threshold o'er;
> But He alone, Who hears my prayer,
>   Hath heard the shutting of the door.

Now I want to suggest that since there is no limit to our imagination, no limited quota of building material, we can have, not just one room, but a whole house. I will tell you about my house of prayer, and you can build your own and furnish it with some of the glorious truths and promises of our faith. And you can use this house of prayer whenever you have a mind to do so. It is easy to memorise the names of the rooms, and you can enter any or all of them as you sit in the corner of a railway carriage, or in the bus or tube on the way to work, or between your home and the station, or even without getting out of bed. This, so far from being lazy, can be a useful place to pray because relaxation is of value and it is easy to relax there. By this method you can stay as long or as short a time as you wish to devote to prayer. There are seven rooms in the house and they are all prayer rooms. Here they are then:

[1] Matthew 5, 15.

Room 1. This is the room in which we *Affirm the Presence of God.* A common objection to prayer is that it "feels like talking to nothing," or that "there is no one there." We cannot engineer feeling, but in the first room let us assert the fact that God is present. This we can do by repeating some of the great texts of the Bible.

All through the Bible God asserts His Presence with His people, and it is real prayer to recall the sentences which recall this to our mind. "Enoch walked with God." "Abraham was the friend of God." To Moses God promised His presence, "Certainly, I will be with thee," and to Joshua He said, "As I was with Moses, so I will be with thee." David feels he can face any dark valley "for Thou art with me," and our Lord not only promised, "Lo I am with you every day until the end of the world," but promised the Holy Spirit "that He may be with you for ever." In this first room I repeat again and again those great words, "with you."

With such passages we "furnish" this room and, of course, we can add to them from the hymn-book and from the poets. Here is a lovely picture from the poems of Rauschenbusch to hang on the walls of this first room:

In the castle of my soul there is a little postern gate
Where, when I enter, I am in the presence of God.
In a moment, in a turning of a thought,
I am where God is.
When I meet God there, all life gains a new meaning,
Small things become great, and great things small,
Lowly and despised things are shot through with glory.

My troubles seem but the pebbles of the road,
My joys seem like the everlasting hills,
All my fever is gone in the great peace of God,
And I pass through the door from Time into Eternity.

Room 2. When we have asserted the fact of the Presence of God, we can pass into the next room in which we *Praise, Thank and Adore God.* It is a good thing to imagine this room full of morning sunshine, for this is the room of thanksgiving. Each of us has something for which to praise and thank God. We can adore Him for all He is in Himself —and, as we do so, we can call to mind His attributes and remember His love, His splendour, His power, His beauty, His holiness. Then we can thank Him for the way he has led us and for all He has done for us. We are to keep our mind—in this room at least—away from our worries and fears and sins. We will look at them later.

We can furnish this room with hymns like the Te Deum and other great hymns of praise from the hymn-book and the poets. I like this prayer:

"Spirit of Life, Who fillest all the world, we worship and adore Thee.

Spirit of Light, Who teachest all the truth, we worship and adore Thee.

Spirit of Beauty, Who dost allow us to rejoice in the works of God, we worship and adore Thee.

Spirit of Holiness, Who dost call us to become sons of God, we worship and adore Thee.

Thou has borne with us so long, bear with us now.

Lord and Giver of life, we worship and adore Thee. Through Jesus Christ our Lord."

Room 3. Now we are ready for a room, rather dim and shadowy as we enter, but brighter as we move across it to the window. It is the room of *Confession and Absolution.* This is the Room of Unloading.

Here we confess our sins, not just in a general way, but really being honest. Most of us are sometimes jealous, malicious, unkind, irritable, proud, intolerant, impure. We pull off the slick business deal and feel a little bit ashamed.

We disparage another's good name. We darken by our depression the brightness of another's life. In a hundred ways we do what we know to be wrong and fail to do what the inner spirit prompted us was right. Terribly often we are indifferent to another's need.

But God is always ready and willing to forgive us. We can move towards the window, pull up the blind and let the streaming light of loving forgiveness and acceptance flood the room. We may feel loved, understood, forgiven, accepted.

In this room Psalm 51 would be a suitable piece of furniture; the Psalm in which David pours out his soul to God and finds pardon. Before we leave this room, too, we must make sure that we are ready to forgive others who may have sinned against us. Nothing is clearer in the New Testament than the fact that God asks not so much a penitence that is complete, as a spirit that will forgive another. "Forgive us our sins, as we forgive them that trespass against us."

Here also we confess our fears and put down our worries and our dark anxieties. They are not necessarily sins. Some of them we cannot help. But here we tell God about them and let the sunshine of His love and purpose shine upon them. Our confusion we put down here, too; our bewilderment as to what we ought to do and which way we ought to go.

Room 4 is set aside for *Affirmation and Reception.* Cleansed by forgiveness we are ready now to receive. This prayer of positive affirmation is important. We are no longer to dwell on the depths to which we have fallen, but on the heights to which God will lead us. God is waiting to give. Jesus put the matter in an unforgettable sentence, "Whatsoever things ye pray and ask for, believe that ye have received them and ye shall have them."[1]

So, quietly, with body and mind relaxed, to myself in this

[1] Mark 11, 24.

room I may say over and over again sentences like: "The Peace of God is mine. God is giving me His power now. In God I am one with the Spirit of Love. I am caught up into His mighty purposes now. I am safe within His care. The Everlasting Arms are round about me and will not let me fall."

Clearly the twenty-third Psalm is part of the furniture of this room. It does not ask, "O Lord, be my Shepherd." It affirms that He is. It does not ask for guidance. It rests in the affirmation that the soul is being guided. "He leadeth me in a true path for His name's sake and He is restoring my soul." Say it over quietly and confidently.

It might help us to remember that if God were not willing to give, then we could wrest nothing out of His hands. But if He is willing to give, then we have only to take. The Bible says He is more willing to give than we are to ask. How *can* I take? I take by affirming that His love and power are at my disposal, and that His peace is flooding my heart, even while I bow in this inner room.

Room 5 is the place for *Purified Desire and Sincere Petition.* We all know what our dominant desires are. In this room we look at them again in the light of God. Maybe we shall see that in that light our prayer to become manager of the bank, or headmistress of the school, to make money, achieve fame or be a social success is not so important as to be used by God in some way that helps others.

It is found that some of our thoughtless and selfish prayers that begin, "I want," die on our lips by the time we get to this room in the house of prayer. Probably by this time we want to love more deeply both God and our fellows and promote God's interests even more than our own. We stop saying, "Give me," and start saying, "Make me" and "Use me." This is the place where we ask for renewed trust and stronger faith and more tolerant love for those who differ from us.

In a university common room a number of lecturers were chatting together. Someone asked the question, "What do you want to be?" The others replied in turn and the answers were not unworthy. One wanted an academic distinction, another an athletic prize, another a professor's chair. One man, shy and sensitive, said quietly, "You fellows will laugh at me, but I want to be a saint." They did not laugh at him. In many ways he is a saint and the most healthy influence on a large American University Campus. When we can sincerely say that, we are purifying our petitions.

Room 6 is that of *Intercession for Others*. It has never seemed practicable to me to spend a lot of time on each person for whom I wish to pray, and if the other rooms in the house of prayer have been conscientiously visited, it seems enough to me to say the name of the person slowly, calling him to mind in as vivid a picture as possible, and then imaginatively *watching him emerging from his difficulties*: being made well—if we are praying about his health, being made confident, courageous, serene, joyous, or whatever it may be. My own plan is to have four lists numbered one to thirty-one and against each numeral to write a name. Then on the day of the month I am praying, I think of the four people whose names are opposite the number which represents the date. Of course, some must be mentioned daily and urgent situations will arise. But I have never felt that "God bless all my friends" is a sufficiently focused prayer, nor can I feel much reality in praying for causes. "God bless the London Missionary Society," let alone "God bless India" would seem to me less valuable than to think of someone—if possible personally known and whose difficulties are real to one—who is working in that field. By some such plan as this one can really pray for one's friends, if it be only once a month, with some sense of sincerity and reality. "I will make mention of you in my prayers," said St. Paul.[1] George Macdonald says, "I will not say that I will pray for you, but I shall think of God and you together."

Room 7 is a big room at the top of the house set aside for *Meditation.* Here we are to take an incident in the Gospels and try to do what Ruskin said he did, imaginatively "to be present as if in the body at each recorded act in the life of the Redeemer." We might indeed work steadily through the Gospels in this way, imaginatively watching the incidents happen and especially "looking at Jesus."

For example, I open my Testament at St. John 3 and see Jesus in an Upper Room having supper privately with Nicodemus. An Easterner often hates being overlooked when eating, so all the shutters are closed. The room gets hot and stifling, and we hear the evening breeze stirring in the grape-vine that climbs up the outside of the house. The meal concluded, I see Jesus move towards the window and speak the lovely words: "The wind bloweth where it listeth, and thou hearest the voice thereof, but knowest not whence it cometh and whither it goeth," and then—as He throws open the shutters—"*SO* is he that is born of the Spirit." Such an action alone makes sense of the word "So." Then I feel the fresh evening breeze sweep into the room. The curtains shiver, the wind floats through another room and then another, for this is the house of a rich man, and far away a door bangs. . . .

Then I ask God to help me open all the windows and doors of my heart so that no room is closed against Him, so that no stuffy pride and unwholesome thoughts may lurk in any secret place, but that His life-giving Spirit may cleanse and refresh and renew every part of the house of life. So my meditation ends—as it should—in dedication. The will should be strengthened by all that the imagination has contemplated.

[1] Romans 1, 9; Ephesians 1, 16.

This sevenfold way may not attract you.   All that matters is that you should find *some* way of praying that is *real*, and neither dull or burdensome, nor so unarranged and desultory as to waste time and be unrewarding.

One could, of course, fill the scheme out to last an hour or more, or shorten it to a few minutes.   It is really rather fun to gather passages from the Bible, the hymn-book, the poets and the essayists and biographers to make more pictures and furniture for each room.   One could in time put up different pictures each day in every room.

At any rate, I pass on the scheme for what it is worth. We need God.   The masters of prayer teach us that all the factors I have mentioned like adoration, thanksgiving, confession, petition, intercession and meditation have their place, and yet some of their books are so advanced that they frighten beginners like me.

We must each find the way.   "God," said Emerson, "enters by a private door into every individual."   But we can help by making an imaginative house with many doors and open them all to Him.   As long as God comes, it does not matter how, but we must give Him a chance.   Even Jesus could not live without God.   How can we expect to do so?

"Behold," He says, "I stand at the door and knock.   If any man hear My voice and open the door, I will come in to him *and will sup with him*"—in the East an unmistakable offer of friendship from which there will never be any turning back.   Let us make a house of prayer and open the door every morning, for to commune with Him may well be the cause for which we were created.   He is the Reality beyond all seeming.   He is the Goal of serious questing.   He is Himself the Answer to all our prayers.

APPENDIX II

HYPOCHONDRIASIS

HYPOCHONDRIASIS, the morbid preoccupation with, and concern about, our own health, in the absence of evidence of serious disease, is a symptom of anxiety. It is not a disease entity of itself. The radical cure is psychological treatment. We must co-operate with the psychiatrist until relentlessly there is laid bare the reason why we are so concerned about our own health. Then we shall be helped to tackle the causative situation. It is important to do this lest our introspective preoccupation and self-concern grow and exclude all other interests. Hypochondriasis *may* be a symptom of a perfectionism. It is as though the patient said, "I am on a pedestal of perfection, and it is intolerable that at any point I am capable of falling below that standard. Physical imperfection, however, is more tolerable than mental or moral, so I will focus my attention and that of others, on that, and divert attention, my own and others, from moral or mental imperfection."

Shelley wrote of "a dark idolatry of self," and Karen Horney in *Neurosis and Human Growth* sees the chief obstacle to growth in the neurotic substitution of a pseudo-self for the real self, and the progressive organisation of life and experience about that false centre. By a process of self-glorification and idealisation, instead of the real-self finding realisation, the mental energies are used up in an attempt to actualise this idealised pseudo-self, and any physical imperfection is anxiety-causing, yet more tolerable than the truth.

Miss Horney writes: "People whose need is to be always

right, feel entitled never to be criticised, doubted or questioned. Those who are power-ridden feel entitled to blind obedience. . . . The arrogant, vindictive person, who is driven to offend others, but yet needs their recognition, feels entitled to 'immunity.' Whatever he perpetrates on others, he is entitled to have nobody mind anything he does. Another version of the same claim is the one for 'understanding.' No matter how morose or irritable one is, one is entitled to understanding! The individual for whom 'love' is the over-all solution, turns his need into a claim for exclusive and unconditional devotion."[1]

This vicious, insidious self-love and the anxiety we develop lest we lose self-esteem produces the symptom of hypochondriasis. It is a symptom present in many so called "nervous" people. Narcissism[2]—so called after the mythical Greek youth of great beauty, Narcissus, who saw his image reflected in a pool and fell in love with himself, ultimately dying of self-love—is a stage through which all human beings pass. But adult maturity should leave it behind. Some people unfortunately suffer from partially arrested personality development, and although other aspects of their personality develop to maturity, they remain childishly in love with themselves, or part of themselves; for example, their voice, or appearance, or their poems or songs or sermons are regarded as "loved projections of themselves." They are "fixated at an infantile level," as we say. Others, threatened by anxiety-provoking stimuli, regress to it. In other words, they make a strategic withdrawal to a more primitive level of personality development, a level on which they need only be concerned with themselves—as a child is. On that infantile level they are free from adult anxiety, and adult responsibilities.

[1] I owe much here to Karen Horney and to Professor John Magee's excellent book, *Reality and Prayer.*
[2] See *Psychology, Religion and Healing*, pp. 422-3 (4th Edition, Hodder & Stoughton, 1954).

Clearly if, at an adult level, one feels anxious, frightened or insecure, it is a relief from these symptoms if one can revert to a childish level on which one did not know such symptoms.   Similarly if one can concentrate one's fear on, say, one organ of the body or, on bodily health in general, then one localises anxiety, and fear of the collapse of the entire ego is withdrawn and made less terrifying.   So one becomes morbid, say, about one's sore throat, or exaggeratedly anxious about one's rheumatism or other non-killing condition, or, if fear is associated with guilt, one develops cancer-phobia or a morbid fear of syphilis, which one will then regard as punishment.   The very fact that one feels one deserves punishment often retains the symptom.

Here again we see the neurotic trend by which the patient *desires* to retain symptoms.   He accepts his hypochondriasis because it is easier to say, "I feel afraid because I'm worried about my throat, or my tummy, or my lungs," than to say, "I feel afraid, but I don't know why and dare not or cannot be bothered to find out why I am afraid."

The patient with hypochondriasis is making a strategic withdrawal to a more secure type of adjustment rather than searching for the true causes of his anxiety, and at the same time he is winning sympathy—"You must be sorry for me, I'm worried about my throat"—or whatever organ it may be.

It is a condition which should be treated by a psychiatrist.

At the risk of being tedious, it is important to add that, of course, if the health is really threatened; if there is good *reason* for supposing that an organ of the body is affected, then the reaction of a certain amount of fear is natural.   This is fear, not anxiety.   (See p. 17.)   But when repeated examinations show no basis for the fear, it may have passed into an anxiety which has a morbid root such as I have indicated.   And even if organic disease is present, an excessive amount of fear is a regressive and narcissistic preoccupation, and thus it is hypochondriacal.

When physical health fails through increasing age we find a person focusing on it thus. "How can they (= I) expect me to maintain my high standard when I am not well?" His anxiety is caused by the desperate fear of being unable to remain at the height of earlier achievement. By focusing his mind on disease, weakness, fatigue, etc., he allows himself a lower standard of attainment, but at the price of symptoms. But he would rather have the symptoms than to be thought to be "going off" without them as his excuse. So he *must* retain them. He would be wiser to (1) Understand the situation; (2) Lessen the demands he makes on himself; (3) Accept a less spectacular output without need of physical excuse for it; (4) Find new ways of self-expression which demanded less emotional output, and follow the other suggestions of this chapter.

As anxiety is sometimes switched to general ill-health, or to disease in some particular organ of the body, so it may be switched to money. The anxious patient gets into a panic by dwelling on the thought that he has insufficient means and will be unable to provide for himself and his family. One friend of mine, though very rich, was certain, during anxiety attacks, that he had lost, or would lose, all his money. He switched his anxiety to money. Anxiety was such a threat to his inner security that the mind found it easier to switch over his fear to outer security. Unconsciously he reasoned, "Now my inner security is threatened I must at least make sure of outward, i.e. financial security. The real origin of the anxiety was finally discovered to be the fear of being found out concerning a comparatively trivial happening which he had surrounded with guilt feelings and repressed. Something approaching a delusion of poverty was produced because the unconscious mind argued thus: "I do not deserve to have money because I have done this wicked thing. My money will, therefore, be taken from me." He was entirely freed from anxiety by uncovering his guilt, making restitution, and accepting the forgiveness of God. To those who have never studied the queer workings of the mind, it sounds strange to say that apparent anxiety about money was cured by the realisation of divine forgiveness, but this is what actually happened.